What Colour Soul is Your Dog?

What Colour Soul is Your Dog?

Kelly MacNeill

A big shout out to Cherie Asher for being an awesome editor, Hannah Carwardine for bringing my illustration ideas to life, Penny Royal for her graphic design skills in putting my cover together along with creating my angel pig and finally, Copy Press for getting me over the line. Arohanui!
Big Love to you all.

Published 2024
by Angel Pig Press

ISBN 978-0-473-72464-1

© Copyright Kelly MacNeill 2024

All rights reserved.

Except for the purpose of fair reviewing, no part of this publication may be reproduced or transmitted in any form or by any means, electronic or mechanical, including photocopying, recording or any information storage and retrieval system, without prior written permission from the publisher.

COPYPRESS

Printed by CopyPress, Nelson, New Zealand.

www.copypress.co.nz

This book is for everyone that has stood with me through the years. For all the lessons learned. Thank you. Humans and animals alike.

Introduction

Kia ora! Kiwi greetings to you.

My name is Kelly, and I am an osteopath. Although at the beginning of writing this book I was not allowed to call myself one (I will explain *that* to you later). This memoir tells only a small part, a single golden thread of my life. Fifteen years of adversity and adventure taking me from maiden to mother. It transports me from my humble beginnings studying osteopathic medicine in the UK, to my present time here in New Zealand, aged 45.

My past was a colourful one, though this is not the time to dwell on those years. I expect there's another wee book there; I'm not sure I have it in me to write it all down yet. I am hampered by writing resistance. It is too fragmented and unsettling, my memories hazy. I shall wait patiently for clearance and clarity. When I reach that stage of my healing, no doubt it will come.

I had a pretty run of the mill childhood and adolescence. By run of the mill I mean alcohol induced crazy, both my parents and me. It hasn't damaged me too much though, and I have it to thank for the completely nonplussed way in which I have embraced all that follows. We have had some trials and tribulations over the years, but one factor remains, I love my family dearly, even if they are a bit bonkers. The environment in which I grew up has helped to shape me into the colourful, intuitive creature I am today.

Growing up, it was not unusual to speak of poltergeist activity and for unexplainable happenings to occur around the house. My mother, with her crystal ball, tarot cards, and ability to perceive beyond the veil, was completely capable of frying the mind of unsuspecting initiates. Night-time was when I could escape. Reading magical fantasy such as *The Magic Faraway Tree* and the partaking of it in my "dreams". I hesitate to call them dreams. Astral travel, where your energetic body leaves your physical body and explores other planes, would be more appropriate.

Often I would fall through a door in the base of a tree and find myself in faery land with all the typical folk one might imagine residing in the land of the fae. I would visit the exact same place each time. I was there, in that place, no doubt about it. Enjoying, it would seem, the world below. The world above explored by flying. I would run, leap, and lift off. Pumping my wings, soaring higher and higher. That I was flying was inexplicably real. Up there in the clouds, the vast landmass far below me, I felt at peace. The ability to visit faraway places at the snap of my fingers, and not just the faraway places of my beloved Enid Blyton. Today, I am eternally grateful that I can still see fae in waking life, all around us. I do not have to sleep to experience them. Those worlds exist whether you see them or not. I see dragons and angels and plant spirits. I sometimes see dead people. And I have wings. Yes, for real. Huge, white angel wings. But don't let me give it away too early.

The spiritual path, in my experience, is not one of direct ascendance, a smooth straight line to enlightenment. It's more of a spaghetti Bolognese affair. We often hear "No growth in the comfort zone," and in my case, I have found this to be most true. I have also found it to be true that "every cloud has a silver lining." There is great strength and courage to be found in adversity and this can make for an exciting life should you dare to step outside of your comfort zone.

I never intended to become an alcoholic, but of course, by the time I had hit my proverbial alcoholic rock bottom, I was already completely dependent. Until my own healing journey began, spirituality could not have been further from my mind. I had never given it a second thought until I was directed, with some force, onto my path of spiritual awakening and personal healing. Maybe you too are a slightly frazzled middle-aged lady with children, ex-husbands, dependency issues, and a dream. I am here to let you know you can do it. You really can. My own dependency issues barely slowed me down. In fact, they may have inadvertently accelerated my spiritual growth. Not that I am advocating alcoholism as a gateway for expanded consciousness, because I absolutely am not. But there is something to be said for the ability to empathise with all walks of life; for having walked in many shoes.

My colourful life has presented many fabulous opportunities to pass through rites of passage. Rites of passage that are taking me from my very own darkness to my very own light. A true path of enlightenment. With every setback, mistake, struggle, another chance to learn and grow. Would you believe that one day you too might take comfort in the trials and tribulations of life? That you too might see them for what they are, great opportunities for change, expansion, ascendance.

We are not people's perception of us. We are not who society has deemed us to be. Hell, we are not even who our parents say we are, or what we perceive of ourselves. We must take back ownership of our mind-blowing personal power. We need to venture deep inside and rediscover our true essence. We each hold the knowledge of the Universe within.

I have spent years embroiled in drama, mostly of my own making. Now, I seek peace. So, who am I really? What am I here to do? For a long time, I did not give these questions any thought whatsoever. Let me prompt *you* to start now.

This is my dream, my calling, my story. So, if you are looking for a little magic and mayhem, or maybe you have your own dependency issues, or are just interested in what someone's spiritual awakening actually looks like, read on.

Chapter 1

My osteopathic odyssey began back in mid-2010. We were having a celebration for a cousin, our buddy Em, who was embarking on a new life in Australia. The children (girls aged 2 and 1) were in bed, and us six or so adults were raucous. It was right here, round the wine and cigarette strewn table, that I had an epiphany.

Everything went quiet – well, the others didn't actually go quiet, they just faded out of my awareness – and a *loud*, god-like voice in my head boomed, "YOU MUST BE AN OSTEOPATH." A literal calling. Holy moly. Then I was back in my awareness, back in our kitchen.

"What the devil is an osteopath?" I asked our party. We continued to drunkenly ruminate over this question long into the night. I am not sure any of us really knew for sure, although Em kind of knew a bit as she had done a massage qualification.

At the time of this epiphany, I was largely a stay-at-home mum to two toddlers but kept my hand in work with the occasional landscaping and garden designing job, my most recent career to date. My husband, Gary, earned enough most of the time to keep a roof over our heads, food in the fridge, and the red wine flowing. Was I really going to start a new career *now*?

In this reincarnation, thus far, I had worked as a paper round girl, pub pot wash, check out girl at our local newsagent and Halfords (auto parts place), barmaid, manager of two London pubs, and an OSG (operational support grade) in prison after failing my officer exams—wrong attitude apparently; I am not suited to a hierarchical environment and would not remove my feet from the table, not even for the Governor.

It wasn't boring though. I did *so* enjoy the bottles of sperm that were frequently launched at me from the high cell windows. Thankfully they missed each time, but it would amuse me to consider how long it might have taken to fill said bottle only to be thwarted at the pinnacle moment of their devious plan.

I had taken the position at HMYOI Aylesbury after returning from my stint living in London running bars in Mornington Crescent (cocaine mafia) and then Commercial Street in the East End (violent gangsters). It was a time of poor choices, irrational decision making, and tumultuous relationships. Enough said, right. My grandad and uncle worked at the prison and lured me there with promises of a job for life, great perks, and a pension. My mum fell for that line and started working there after me – she is still there, hanging on for the moment she can retire. This bird, though, was not for caging, and I walked after a couple of years.

I never really found my swing until I went back to college and studied for three years to gain a BTEC in Garden Design and Horticulture. I loved it. It was in my blood. Much of my childhood was spent around the family nursery. My dad and uncles were nursery men and landscapers themselves. I became a garden designer and landscaper in my own right, with my own firm. I extolled the virtues of having women on site and took full advantage of our standing in a male dominated profession by always securing first deliveries of the day. This was achieved by wearing scant clothing on site during summer.

Those days were wholly hedonistic, mad, wild, and free. My best Kiwi friend Claire, who worked with me, will attest to this. We would tear around in my Ford Transit Tipper, bikini top or crazy hat depending on the weather, cigarette hanging from our chops, looking forward to meeting up with the lads in the local pub at the end of the day. It was outrageously crazy, but working every day out in nature, handling the plants, and having my hands in the soil, went some way to keeping me sane.

The transition from maiden to mother at the age of 28 was a massive shock to the system, and for a long time, I mourned the loss of wild, free me. With time, I adjusted. I was far less wild, or so I thought ... glimpses could still be had. Some might say more than glimpses if you were to ask, but it would depend on who you asked. Some might say hedonistic, some might say dependent. Sure I was sometimes so wild I passed out early and someone else had to look after the children, but I was just having fun.

It wasn't all like that though. I had a veggie garden; I was the queen of ginormous cabbages. I baked bread. We had chooks. We still threw the odd party, but life was fairly sedate in a mummies that wine kind of way.

A friend enquired how long I could keep it up. We only ever drank wine and partied together. I still don't know if she drinks tea or coffee and we have been friends for a very long time. It was only ever wine unless I was on a really well-behaved streak, then she drank wine and I drank a substitute whilst trying to extol the benefits of not drinking. This often fell on deaf ears, hers and mine, and it wouldn't be long until we were both back drinking wine together. She knew though that being a stay-at-home mummy was not for me long term. I had always craved excitement, spontaneity; I had too much energy.

And she was right. Change was upon me once more. A positive one though. I had had a bona fide calling! A proper otherworldly voice had called to me. Who knew it worked that way. The divine actually shouting at you. Maybe the divine had lost patience with me, maybe I was often too drunk to hear. Maybe I had needed an *extra loud* calling.

I was so grateful and very excited – like an exuberant puppy. It was something that would take me out of the monotony of early motherhood. Nothing would stop me. I would be a mother *and* I could study for a degree. The divine had decreed it so.

Do not get me wrong. I loved being a mother to my two girls, and as was ever the case, alcohol helped ease the boredom, it had done so through many situations over the years. Happy, sad, bored, angry, anxious. You name it, any excuse, alcohol helped them all. I would have to slow down now if I was to study. No party party. Serious, studious Kelly now. Hallelujah.

My calling was so forthright. The forward driving momentum was intense. There was no getting away from it. There was no other way. I was to be an osteopath. And would you have it, what seemed like an absolute impossibility was made absolutely possible within the month. It was incredible. Divinely guided you could say.

Chapter 2

The days following the calling were a whirlwind of exploring the world of manual therapies. I compared osteopathy, physiotherapy, and chiropractic in as much depth as my patience would allow, about a day's worth of Google. I learned they all used massage, joint articulation, and joint mobilisation to varying degrees. I did not know anything else about any of them really, and my research was wholly unnecessary anyway.

Even though I had never visited one, or even knew what one was, the calling towards osteopathy was too strong. There was no chance of deviating from the osteopathic path laid out so loudly in my head. I had never even had anyone lay hands on me in a remotely healing way. Never even been for a massage. As a landscaper I used to wake with a sore back every morning. Never even considered that someone might be able to help me with that. I was that unaware.

What I know now is that osteopathy is a practical hands-on healing touch modality that considers body, mind, and spirit when looking for health within a patient. Dis-ease in any of these realms will likely cause dis-ease within another. We know that the health status of any of our individual parts affects how our divine machine, our body, works as a whole. Who we surround ourselves with, our attitude, what we do day in and day out, what we put into our systems all affects our health status. Fortunately for us, the body, mind, and spirit are capable of many remarkable endeavours. You may not realise it, but given the right tools, we are able to fix more from within than we give ourselves credit for. The osteopath knows this and utilises it. They help you find your health.

You can see an osteopath for just about anything you like. They come in many different flavours though, so if you are unsure about your symptoms, just ring one and ask. We all grow our toolboxes at different rates and favour different tools. You might have to shop around to find the one with the right tools for your uniquely divine machine. If someone's name keeps popping up, you probably need to see them. The Universe is handy like that.

There is definitely diversity within osteopathy. A scale so to speak. Some coming from a very practical, physical standpoint, with others coming from a very spiritual viewpoint and everyone in between. There is no right or wrong, better or worse. There is only what is, and what there is, is someone for everyone. We are all valid and all needed. It all depends on where you are on your journey and what you need in the present moment.

Now that I had some basic information, even if it wasn't needed, I now looked to where to study. Bearing in mind we had zero, and I mean *zero*, funds. I think it was also around this time that my husband's workplace had gone bankrupt, and we were living on housing benefits and the dole. Deep joy.

I researched all the institutions that offered osteopathy degrees and it soon became clear that I would have to study the four-year full-time course over five years, they called it fully part time, to allow for me to still work at times (how we laugh at this one, no actual chance) and see the family (only slightly more chance).

There were not many institutions offering this pathway, and the logical thing was to chase up the nearest one: The College of Osteopaths in Borehamwood, Hertfordshire, UK, about 45 minutes Northwest of Central London and 40 minutes southeast from our home. As luck would have it, I was not far off the intake deadline of September 2010. I arranged myself for an interview and off I went.

Now, I'm not well known for thinking things through in their entirety, more acting on explosive impulse. I once lost my driving license for driving under the influence. I sold my newly imported Mercedes Smart car to pay the car loan off in one hit, but they did not allow early settlement. So, I promptly blew the money on a load of shite. Then I went on a drink awareness course and got my license back early and wished I still had the car. When it came to looking for colleges I hadn't given too much thought to the fact that although I had the level of qualification they were looking for, the subjects were a bit off the mark, namely horticulture and garden design. However, I went forth armed with little more than the unwavering belief that all would be well. After all, I was the genuine recipient of a Calling. I was divinely guided. No drama.

I can still remember that interview. A panel of three interviewers, myself sat in front of them, took place upstairs in a back room of the training clinic, a converted 1930s two story family home. It did not seem appropriate to tell them that I had had a calling and until recently had not known what an osteopath was. But if I could explain to them how my horticulture qualifications and skills were transferable to an Osteopathic Degree, I would be in. I proceeded to blather something along the lines of tactility, all living things, our health in relation to the food we grew, the natural world. I was pleased they were humouring me. And then voila! I was an osteopathic student. I'm not even really sure how it happened, but I was due to start in a couple of weeks. In hindsight, it was a natural progression from student of the land to student of the body, so entwined are they, but in reality, I still knew bugger all.

I didn't even make it home to tell hubby. I was so excited, I called him on the way. I remember it went something like this ...

Me: "Hey hun, I got accepted onto the osteopathic course!"

Gary: "That's great. How the frak are we going to afford that?"

Me: "It's okay, I already thought of that and put the car on Autotrader."

There was no finance available for my chosen degree path, even though it was my first degree. To qualify, you had to do the full-time degree, not a viable option for our family. The first-year fees of approximately £5,000 were due immediately. We could spread the cost over the year but the fee would be higher. Being skint, that's the path we took. That's the path we would take for the next five years, with the fees going up and up each year, naturally. We still thought the five year, fully part-time degree would give us a life outside of studying and the option to earn some money to pay for it and everything else having a family entails.

Osteopathy was, and probably still is viewed as quite a middle-class profession. I'm sure many of the largely mature students already had well-paying jobs, savings, or were able to remortgage their homes. Well, we had no savings, and we lived in a council house; I was not working much due to the fact of having two small girls; and hubby's boss had gone bankrupt.

On the upside, and you will learn this of me, there is *always* an upside (it drives my teenagers insane), hubby was not long out of work, just a blip thankfully. Plus we sold our car, a Toyota Landcruiser, fully pimped V8 sex machine (which, if truth be told, we could not afford to run, but it did look and sound good) for a Citroen Picasso which had been owned for many years by a chain-smoking commuter, and the first-year fees were in the bag. I may have cried a little at this point but Gary cleaned it up a treat.

The required financial cost did not stop at the fees. There was of course uniform, books, travel expenses, yada, yada.

"Don't worry," I'd tell hubby, "the Universe will provide." He sure had some choice answers to that little sentiment. I'm positive he thought he was the one providing.

≋ ★ ≋

Ahhhh, my first year as a mature student. I loved it.

I can still remember my first lecture. The tutor standing there with a femur in his hands, unbeknown to me at the time, a reference to the Osteopathic Jedi Master that is Andrew Taylor Still. "Welcome everyone" – there may have been more embellishment to his welcome, but this is what sticks in my mind – "Could everyone please dress down to their underwear." Nervous giggles … all looking around … an even mix of mostly mature men and women. We didn't know each other from Adam. "Don't be shy now. This is how you will spend most of your time, so best get it out of the way."

It was in the back of my mind that we would probably have to undress at some point with it being a hands-on treatment modality – you know, where you actually have to look at and touch other people's bodies in order for them to get better – I just hadn't expected it on the first day. I would have appreciated some warning. I rarely shave or wear a bra, but it must have been everyone's lucky day. I was hairy, but at least I had a sports bra on. Hairy nipples covered. Phew.

My first day in the training clinic is another day that will stay with me. After meeting Lin, our clinic manager, any notions of grandeur were swiftly knocked out of me. Off I went in my new white clinic coat feeling ever so important. You know what I did in the first few weeks? Nothing but filing. Sure, I probably got to observe a few patients, but it was mostly just filing. I not so silently fumed at Lin, but I was eternally grateful for the lesson.

In the clinic environment, there is no hierarchy. Everyone and every job is an important cog in the smooth functioning of the clinic, and *nobody* was above filing. I had to pull out every file and determine by the last date the patient came in whether their file could be moved upstairs where it was filed again. After I completed the hundreds, if not thousands, on the ground floor, I then went through all the ones upstairs to determine if they were indeed filed correctly – all in alphabetical order. My inner control freak meant that this had to be done correctly, no half-heartedness, no skimping. Bugger. It sure did teach me an important lesson on the efficient storage of patient notes plus extreme gratitude for automated notes when they came. I came to love Lin, too. She was the heart and soul of that place.

And so it would go for the next five years: leaving the family on the weekends, driving, or getting the train to London and getting my kit off for the university lectures, and getting to Borehamwood teaching clinic for observation and workshops during the week. We would not get our hands on actual patients until the third year though.

Those first years were spent mastering anatomy and physiology, so much anatomy and physiology my brain bled, and of course lots of hands on each other. You quickly became very intimate with your cohort, which did help us gain massage and articulation qualifications over those first two years – a by-product of our osteopathic training. This was great, it meant that we could get hands on the unsuspecting public and get paid for it.

In the beginning it's not as easy as you might think, to put your hands on a stranger's naked flesh. Most of us needed a fair bit of practice. As we learnt all the different muscles, ligaments, and tendons, we learnt how to manipulate them, what different strokes achieved and why, what pressure to use, and when and how to move and mobilise joints. The first two years of an osteopathic degree makes you a pretty competent massage therapist.

With all the study and the travel for the clinic and the lectures, I was not able to give a lot of time to my landscaping business. We desperately needed money, so I sold my van and tools and chucked the money in the study pot. When I gained the massage and articulation certificate, it made sense to put it to use. Ever the entrepreneur, in 2012 I set up as a massage therapist. I was able to earn money, gain experience, and work around the family.

It is amazing how quickly the year rolls round and another small fortune is needed to secure your place on the course. During these early days, we pretty much sold everything that we had of any value. Poor Gary sold his watches and any gold jewellery. It was right amidst the gold boom, so we were fortunate to get good prices for what really were a few gold bracelets and rings. With me now able to work more, the need to sell our things diminished.

I made myself a website and set up in our front room. Stoked to get my first client, I left the room whilst he undressed and returned to find him completely naked. Mmmm, not my bag fella, clothes on and off you go. I had to rethink on the working from home scenario. For some reason, most likely driven by the possibility of earning a premium, I set up a "Mobile Massage 4 U" gig. This went quite well for a short while, catering for the wealthy of nearby Berkhamsted, until one evening, on visiting a couple, it became clear they expected a three-way kind of deal. Also not my bag. I needed to get thinking about how I could market myself as a *proper professional*.

As it happens, around 2013, the beginning of my third year, my good friend Jude, who ran a clinic in Hemel Hempstead, rang me. Their osteopath was on sick leave, could I go and cover? Well, I could not call myself an osteopath yet of course, but I could be a manual therapist for all intents and purposes. I loved that clinic and stayed there beyond qualifying. That's not to say I did not encounter some strange ones.

"I've booked you in a full body massage," Gillian, the clinic manager, informed me one day. The fella was a bit strange, and it became clear as the appointment progressed that he thought he was in a brothel (I found out later that there had been one next door many moons ago but had since closed). I informed him that was not the case and that it would still be £50 and there would be no happy ending. Did he want to continue? Yes, he did. Unfortunately he performed his own happy ending in the toilet after. Eeeeew. I don't think I could have loved Gillian anymore when she cleared up after that excitable bugger.

Life went on. By the time Year 3 was upon us, we unfortunately lost the Citroen Picasso. It had turned out to be a great car. Excellent 2.0 litre diesel engine, so many gizmos and gadgets, little snooks and hiding places, it was like the Tardis. I was saddened when the engine caught fire one winter's day, early in that third year, whilst defrosting on the driveway. It was sold for a pittance to someone who worked for Citroen who said they did that, a "common fault" apparently. We now had a Vauxhall Corsa. A clever little eco diesel, great for running up and down the M25.

The start of Year 3 also saw fewer students in our class. For some, the realisation of how much work was involved saw them leave; some struggled flying in from abroad; and for some it was just too hard. Those of us who remained were a solid crew. I remember at the beginning a tutor touted the average dropout rate, of course that wouldn't be any of us now. I absolutely knew it wouldn't be me; I have a rather unhealthy work ethic (better now), the desperate need to complete stuff and an ungodly amount of sheer bloody mindedness. Another interesting statistic we were told was that due to the pressure of the course, a few of our marriages wouldn't make it. Well, obviously that would not be Gary and me.

Adding to the stress of it all were the exams and presentations that rolled around continuously. Oh, the horror of those practical exams! I used to take an inordinate number of Calms and Bach Flower remedies to still my nerves. The only thing was, I just got more and more crazy. I hadn't realised yet that I was absorbing everyone's anxiety. By the time my turn came, I was a gibbering wreck whose mind would go blank whenever questioned. It didn't help that there was a particular tutor whose energy was the other end of the spectrum from my own and could turn me into a puddle as soon as they looked at me. With hindsight, the best performing practical exams of those early days were the ones where I was a bit hungover from the night before. Not enough to render me incapable, just enough to take the edge off the accumulated hysteria.

Chapter 3

Each year, the amount of time we were required to spend in the clinic went up. We had to accumulate 1,200 clinical hours by the end of the degree. By the beginning of Year 3, I think a few people, me included, were guilty of nodding off a few times in observation. We were chomping at the bit to get hands on. Year 3 was when it intensified ... in some spectacular and interesting ways. We would begin to learn the art of high velocity thrust (HVT) and we would also get our hands on real-life patients.

Now, I am extraordinarily flexible, and there was one tutor who would be at pains to demonstrate to the class that it was possible to crack (HVT) a very flexible person. An HVT involves taking a joint to the end of its range of movement using appropriate planes of movement for the joint, i.e side bending, rotation, flexion or extension, and then moving through the end of range with a quick thrust to re-establish range of movement and decrease pain, among other things which we won't go into here. What is it they say? KISS. Keep It Simple Stupid.

Early on, I was absolutely amazed after one tutor adjusted my sacroiliac joint (SIJ), linking pelvis and sacrum, through HVT, and years of back pain just fell away. Back pain that I paid no heed to but was there every single morning for years. I just put it down to the heavy lifting at work. Amazing. I was hooked. And lucky I was because you needed those skills to qualify.

By the end of five years I left not wishing to be cracked ever again. Now some time has passed and my stance has softened. Take today for example, my awesome friend and colleague Alf adjusted (HVT) my neck and this story just fell out. I had been wanting to start it for ages, but I felt stuck. A nice upper cervical (neck HVT) shift and boom, off we go. Cheers Alf.

≋ ★ ≋

I soon noticed what wasn't discussed was the spiritual aspect of osteopathy. Which is strange in itself because of the four founding principles of osteopathy:

1. The body is a unit; the person is a unit of body, mind, and *spirit*.
2. The body is capable of self-regulation, self-healing, and health maintenance.
3. Structure and function are reciprocally interrelated.
4. Rational treatment is based upon an understanding of the basic principles of body unity, self-regulation, and the interrelationship of structure and function.

Thankfully, the cranial clinic went some way to address this. Now, I'm not going to go into this too much, but cranial osteopathy is a branch of osteopathy that students may get to touch on towards the end of their degree. Or their learning institution may have more of that flavour to them. But it really is more of a postgraduate training. Something to get your teeth into, if you're that way inclined, after you've been out in the real world for a bit, honing your skills. To be honest, all the structural (anatomy and physiology) stuff is enough to get your head around during the actual degree, and many do not have the head space to accommodate it at university. It is akin to learning how to take an airplane into space when A) You didn't realise they could go into space and B) you are only just learning how they are built. Sometimes there's only so much one can absorb at any given time. Not me though. I loved it. I had come home.

Cranial dives into the esoteric portion of osteopathy. Sure, it is still grounded in anatomy and physiology, but at a much deeper level. In essence, bone, muscles, ligaments and tendons are pretty superficial. Although it is marvellous to be able to feel them in their entirety, imagine what it would be like to be able to feel the very essence of the bones, muscles, ligaments or tendons. How about the ability to feel much deeper than these tissues. How about feeling the flow of the fluids and the inherent motion of the organs. It is easier to individuate the systems for learning purposes – cardiovascular, respiratory, digestive, lymphatic, etc – but how many grasp that there are no separate systems at all. Imagine that you could sense, feel, or actually see the oneness of all. To know that we are all made up of zillions of molecules and the only separation, definition of self, others, inanimate stuff, is the lens through which we look and interpret this data or how our brain perceives this information. This takes us one step further into the realms of biodynamic (energetic) cranial osteopathy.

We all know everything is energy right? How can this help us though? Well, as fanciful as this sounds, if you can tune into another person's system, or as I intuitively do, and become one with their system, not only can you see and feel what is happening in your patient but you also become a channel for the divine. Although, as the osteopath, we can see and feel the dysfunction in a person's system, it is not us who makes the change but the inherent wisdom of the person's system. This is what makes us biodynamic cranial osteopaths. We work with the primary respiratory mechanism. Secondary respiration is what goes in and out of your mouth and nose. Primary respiration is the Breath of Life, the Breath of the Universe. When this is lacking in any tissue, you will not be operating from your place of highest potential. With time and training, or in my case an innate reactivated gift, we can feel this lack of breath, and we can feel it return when we give and hold space for it. And when it does return, it brings health with it.

At our college we had a cranial clinic every Friday, and we were allowed to observe from the first year. If you have ever been to a cranial treatment, you will understand that this can be very boring to watch. To the uninitiated it looks static and unexciting, especially for a new, clueless student chasing the excitement of an HVT. More often than not, the patient lays fully clothed on their back on the treatment table. The clinician will put their hands on a part of the patient's body – often head, sacrum, or ankles – and then to the unknowing they will just sit there for 40 or so minutes. Occasionally they might change position. In Year 3 I finally got to put hands on. Not that I needed to put hands on to feel the changes in the patient's system; I could feel them from where I was sitting observing. The Friday cranial clinic was my favourite.

During these sessions, the tutor has hands on with you and guides the treatment. Really the Universe guides it but that might be a bit too much for the average third year student. You are merely there to observe. With hands on in this manner, my world view expanded exponentially, and lovely Ercilia, who was the cranial tutor at the time, became my cranial mentor.

Of course, I already knew that things happened in a cranial treatment, I had received cranial treatments from the beginning of my study and if there was an exciting session to be watched it would be when I was receiving treatment. Where the patient is normally laid comfortably throughout the session, peaceful and relaxed on their back, I would often look as if I was having a fit. I would have convulsions, my teeth would chatter, and I would contort myself into weird shapes and positions, all of which I had absolutely no control over. I knew little of traumatic patterns then. What I hadn't fully grasped at the time was that the tutor was holding space for my system to work out or integrate trauma that it had carried within itself for years. Years of alcohol and substance abuse and the repressed emotion that went along with it was being released and this evidently was not a peaceful transition for my system.

I vividly remember one session when an old habit came back to visit. I had not taken cocaine in years, but as my sinuses were worked on, it was clearly cocaine that ran down the back of my throat. The taste is very distinctive. I'm normally very relaxed after treatment, but that day I remained quite peppy. I have not had to use a nasal decongestant since.

My first treatment also took my breath away. I literally stopped breathing. Or I should say stopped breathing through my nose and mouth, secondary respiration. I felt completely comfortable, natural and at ease. Another mechanism came to the fore. I could feel the expansions and contractions through my physical self and beyond. The expansion and contraction of everything. I was at one with the Universe, primary respiration. The Breath of Life had touched me and I would not look back.

We did have some early cranial study lectures to give us a taste of it and practiced on each other. I remember one session very clearly. A friend and fellow student put his hand on my sacrum, my body lifted into bridge pose, and I couldn't return to the treatment couch. I was stuck. After that session, students were no longer allowed to practice cranial osteopathy on me. It was not to be trifled with.

I almost hesitate to write this, the feeling of my first cranial treatment of another at the training clinic. I can still feel all the sensations as if it were yesterday. The day my path was truly cemented. No going back. My lovely college mentor holding the persons head, and I, in observation, holding the persons ankles. My mentor talking, asking me not to focus, to keep my attention wide, but her words drifted off. I was gone! I was in the person already.

No sooner had I touched their ankles than I felt myself whooshing into the person on the couch. I had my eyes closed but I felt as if my physical body had shifted, that I was somehow flopping over the patient. Mad. I could feel my heart rate rise; I felt anxious and slightly fearful. I could feel beads of perspiration forming. But hang on, these sensations were not mine, they were the patients, and I could feel them in me! In shock, I opened my eyes, but I had not physically moved. I was still sat at the patient's feet, quietly holding their ankles, but there was nothing quiet about this treatment, my other senses had shown me that.

"Holy Moly," I exclaimed. "Can you feel that?" I think my tutor knew from that point on we would be in for some exciting times.

I became a firm favourite of the cranial clinic and attended as many Fridays as I possibly could in those last three years. Cranial clinic became exciting, and I realised other students were keen to come in the treatment room if I was there. We were also able to choose an elective, and of course I chose cranial to attempt to understand the mechanism at work here. I had so many questions, my palpatory skills already far beyond that of the average student in those respects.

To answer some of my questions, my lovely mentor arranged for me to attend some postgraduate lectures on the subject, and for that I am eternally grateful. I loved those sessions – lots of people with the same interest and well on their own journeys to discover their own truths. It was an honour to practise with these accomplished osteopaths; to be told that I have clearly done this in previous lifetimes; to be told that I was not an "ordinary" osteopath and I should not settle for the "ordinary" path. Who defines ordinary anyway? I was stoked. What third year student wouldn't be.

I spent my time there deep diving into people's souls, the room full of people raising the vibration until I literally hummed, everyone hummed. Through all this though, I still had the pivotal sense that we truly did not need to understand the mechanics at play. Our minds could not break it down, put it into words, compartmentalise it, rationalise it. We only had to know it, trust it, be at one with it, and all would be well.

At this point, I was told that it was okay. I could go on and be a healer and there was nothing wrong with that. That what I was perceiving was not what they were teaching and I could follow a different path. Yet I knew we were all perceiving the same thing. It all comes from the same source. I just didn't have the same inclination to break it down. My brain didn't work that way. But I so desperately wanted to be an osteopath. I knew I was an osteopath. My whole belief system was, and still is, based on the osteopathic principles.

I continued to attend postgraduate workshops whilst studying for my degree, but I still needed more, I just wasn't sure what. What these postgrads showed me though, was that I needed to ground myself and level up my energetic self-care. It was abysmal. I was clearly very ungrounded; I spent a lot of my time in the upper worlds. I loved the sensation of flying around. I was nervous that if I grounded myself that I would stop seeing and feeling all the extraordinary, and I did not want that to happen. I was so open energetically; I attracted a lot of unwanted spiritual attention. I needed some spiritual guidance.

Chapter 4

Being able to perceive things that others may not wasn't a new concept to me, my own childhood had seen me well in this regard. But now I could see all sorts of things all over the place, and my life became quite hectic. There was no escape, and I would often have a kitchen full of deceased people wanting me to pass messages on, but this wasn't my thing. I didn't have the facility to contact folk. I couldn't help them, and I had not yet mastered the skill to shift them on. I just needed to get the kids' fish fingers cooked, could they all please leave me alone! It was as though the flood gates had opened and for a time, I had all the extrasensory abilities at my fingertips. I was at a crossroads where I must decide the direction in which I wanted to go. This of course, was predestined. I was to use my gift for healing through osteopathy.

On attending a funeral for one of my husband's uncles, I saw his uncle as we approached the house. He came like in a film still. I had never met him but confirmed it when I saw his picture on the coffin. My husband asked me why I was smiling during the service. I could see passed over folk dancing happily up and down the aisle. To be sitting there happy as Larry is not socially acceptable when people are newly grieving.

One time, I left a crematorium as I was being overwhelmed. I went to sit on a nearby bench to wait for the service to finish and got chatting to a young girl. After a few minutes, realisation dawned.

"You're not alive, are you?"

"No," she said.

She was sweet to pass the time with, and the others stayed away. My favourite of these experiences though was making my way to a friend's mothers funeral. I had known the mother well, and as the hearse passed me on the hill, I heard her clear as day greet me as usual in her distinct cheery northern accent.

I also remember another time, returning from a funeral, it became abundantly clear something had returned with us. Something which may not have had our best intentions at heart. As Gary and I lay in bed that night, I was fixed on something over his shoulder in our bedroom doorway.

"Somethings here isn't it," he said (he had his own spidey senses).

"Yep, sorry hun." Not to worry though. The light within me rose instinctively, filling me up, brimming over and then boomed through our immediate surroundings, like a sonic wave. That sorted that.

At the time, to limit the bonkers, I made a vow to stay away from future funerals wherever possible.

So, as you can see, my life levelled up on the excitement Richter scale. Some folks I didn't mind hanging around. As I journeyed up and down the M25, still in the Vauxhall Corsa, I would often have a slightly over-excited American Indian join me. He would chat and dance and generally do what I felt was his very best to distract me whenever possible. He also became a great source of comfort. I liked him with me, and he stayed right through those final years when things became somewhat tumultuous.

In the study clinic, I would regularly see a large eye watching over us. I would have visions as we worked. I could see and feel the energy fields. The lovely sensation of becoming one with the patient and one with the Universe. Where there were no boundaries and potentials were infinite. I was keen to learn but still struggling with the perceived need to understand what was happening. To be able to define it somehow. I knew it was the truth, the universal truth. I knew that any outcome for the patient was in no way related to my abilities as an osteopath, maybe only my ability to connect to the universal source of light and for the Universe to work its magic through me. I had become a vessel of light.

As a student, I struggled if a deceased relative of the patient showed up in the treatment session. It's not really the expected thing when one attends for a discounted osteopathic session at the local training clinic to also receive a psychic medium session thrown in. It wasn't really covered in the "managing patient expectation" portion of the syllabus or "professional conduct" or "scope of practice". Sometimes my eyes would be on stalks, or my eyebrows would be high on my forehead in surprise, but I mostly kept it to myself. Lin, the practice manager, was an awesome confidant, and a couple of the tutors knew what was going on.

The one thing that I did have to work hard on reigning in, which was freaky to observers but instinctual for me, was the tendency for my eyes to roll back and slip into a trance. Not good when you are running to a clinic schedule. You can easily lose time in this state. Plus, when I do that, I struggle to recall what has happened and that makes it frustrating writing the notes up. Nowadays, if someone shows up in session, I comment. They wouldn't show up if the person present was not ready to receive this information. That does not mean that I can call people up at will, because I don't. You need to see a medium for that.

Still though, I would often return home with tales of the extraordinary. I was still working at the clinic in Hemel Hempstead and had become quite popular – nobody cared that I couldn't call myself an osteopath due to not having yet qualified. Results were being had, and people were happy. So was I, what a huge leap in my osteopathic evolution. My little clinic room became quite crowded as all manner of other world folk joined me in our sessions. I remember one session where angels filled the room. What a sheer honour and delight. When I got home that evening, I remember Gary asking me about the washing up. The f**king washing up. How can he even ask such questions when I have just returned from heaven? Quite literally. How bloody mundane.

Wow, ego again. I really needed to get a handle on this. I couldn't spend *all* my time in the upper worlds and forget that I had a family here, on this plane, which was also real and needed attention. Nobody was above the washing up. I should have learnt from my filing experience.

Chapter 5

In a bid to get a handle on things pertaining to self-care in the energetic world, I looked outside of the college for some help. I knew I needed it.

It was at the beginning of the third year that I began another course run through The Healing Trust, formerly The National Federation for Spiritual Healers, alongside my osteopathy degree. It is the most prominent healing group in the UK and one of the most highly respected and professional spiritual healing organisations worldwide. The healing course was great. My teacher Hertha was great, a lovely lady who appeared to exist solely on grapes and light and who was running parts one and two of the course in London at the time.

I learnt the chakra system and energy fields inside out. I learnt to ground myself, no imagination needed. I could see the twirling branches and roots of the trees growing through me and deep into the ground. I couldn't move if I tried during these exercises. I learnt to meditate, who knew sitting still could be so exciting. I remain a little lazy though; I like guided meditations, laying down. I learnt how to give healings in The Healing Trust format. I learnt the importance of grounding, attuning, asking permission and protection when working, these processes are automatic now.

I remember telling Hertha that I was having extreme pressure in my head.

"Not to worry," she reassured me. "It's just your crown chakra opening."

Not a brain tumour then. *No.* She was quite firm on this.

I cannot pinpoint the exact moment it happened, my head feeling as if it would simultaneously implode and explode, but it was in direct relation to my osteopathic mentor Ercilia giving me a treatment. I distinctly remember the feeling of my head opening wide, and light energy rushing in and flowing out of my hands. The pressure eased in my head to be replaced by a new sensation of a vortex at my crown. Now I just had a burning desire to run around and put hands on everyone. I could feel when people were sick just being in the same vicinity as them, walking past them in the street, bumping into them at the supermarket. The energy built up in such a way that I would need to discharge into something, someone.

One of my favourite places was across the road from our house, in the middle of the farmer's field. There was a little dell that he had left wild and in it grew a gnarly old tree. I'm not even sure what species it was, but it called to me when this happened. I have always been able to see the energy fields of trees, but this was different. I would put my hands on the tree, and I could feel inside the tree. Our energetic fields became one. I could feel the flow in and flow out as the tree grounded me, cleared the energetic build up and rebalanced me. I was so grateful to that tree. In return I would clear the tree.

I got a perceived handle on it, on myself. It gave what I was feeling and experiencing a frame of reference and a grounding of my experiences. I *felt* more grounded. I could see the benefits of remaining grounded when flying around had seemed so exciting. By remaining grounded I had access to further realities. The world above, the world below, *and* all the worlds beyond. The Universe.

I say perceived as I'm not sure you ever really have a handle on it. Just when you think you have it sussed the Universe sends another curve ball. Sure, I was still a bit of a noisy menace in the healing class, over excited to feel and move energy, I would whoop with delight. I loved learning how to clear the energy centres, make sure they were spinning the right way and emitting their life-giving light. I had it mastered in about five minutes, the practical doing of it. So simple and very effective. Not the be all and end all but a big cog in the energetic wheel and something that needs to be addressed when looking at a person holistically.

Learning as I went, I was advised by a colleague that I should not be walking around so energetically open and that there was a technique to close the energy centres. I considered that maybe this would be a good idea and would also lessen the amount of unwanted spiritual attention I may receive if I were to continue to remain open to all. So I tried this a few times, the closing of my centres, and nearly vomited. So much nausea rolled through me. Closing my energy centres was not for me and I remain wholly open to this day with a constant sensation of the light coming in through my crown. I relish this feeling of connection to the whole.

With time and experience, I can now easily discern what is mine and what is not; what I wish to engage with spiritually or not. I can stand apart from others drama but am ever vigilant as it is easy to get sucked in. I am having a human experience after all. I have better protection in place and energetic maintenance for myself. I walk barefoot on the ground; I swim in natural bodies of water. I constantly return to my midline, ground myself, and endeavour to speak and act from that place of connectedness.

Over that year, I completed parts one and two of the four-part Healing Trust course. I had needed Hertha's guidance during that time, and she helped me enormously. Teachers always appear at the right time. I would not return to complete parts three and four until after my degree had finished (2015). I could not bear to leave the course unfinished even if I felt it was a box ticking exercise – ego again, such a bugger. I was so sad to learn when I did return to finish that Hertha was no longer teaching for the Trust. I finished parts three and four during 2016 and 2017 with a lovely lady named Sue.

I offered to treat Sue's husband who had been pottering. I went through the process of grounding, attuning, asking for permission and protection before the laying on of hands. The Healing Trust works off-body but in this instance, I put hands on. It is as natural to me as breathing. I slipped easily into an altered state energetically, dividing my attention. I am here but I am there. Present, yet not. In the next instant, the largest, most beautiful pair of angel wings unfurled between this gentleman's shoulder blades. Enormous wings that extended above his head and down the back of his calves. Whiter than white. He flexed them, they had been curled up a while, they needed a stretch.

"Typical," said Sue, "I'm the healer and he gets the wings."

I hope he maintains those beautiful wings. You don't just get them and then that's it. They are just part of the infinite process of levelling up, clearing your energy centres, raising your vibration across lifetimes.

My own etheric wings resurfaced during this exciting time. I had previously only felt my wings during times of sleep where I would leave my physical body, run along the ground, and then fly high. I still have these very real flying episodes. The process was aided, I believe, by the removal of physical restrictions in my upper thoracic spine. I had long had a nagging pain at the level of T3/T4, the third and fourth vertebrae of the thoracic spine which also contributes to the neural innervation of the heart. We cleared these restrictions during classes whilst learning about mobilization and manipulation of the spine. I remember the feeling of mass expansion through my energy field as a T4 restriction was removed.

After this instance, I was helping Gary with a headache; I remember feeling his headache in myself. Having swapped bedrooms with the children as they were unsettled, it became apparent that something quite dense was present and was perched at the bottom of our bed. I noticed the entity, dark and crouching. It leapt towards us. It was the shape of a compact medium sized dog with snarling jaws and strong sharp claws. I did not feel afraid in the slightest – I rarely feel afraid during supernatural experiences. In a flash, a giant pair of angel wings unfurled from between my shoulder blades and wrapped themselves around us both. Ooooh, hello wings. A sonic boom swept through the room. Bye, bye entity.

I must be mindful to nurture my own wings, and the easiest way to do that is to nurture myself: body, mind, and spirit. I can feel my wings move when I pull energy or breathe through my heart centre (sternum). I can tune into them at will, but they are most prominent when I am treating. They will often expand to their full size at the end of a session and, as you have just read, when spiritually threatened, which is a rarity thankfully.

Other sensitives can see them, and young children can see them, too. I can flex my wings and the child's eyes widen like saucers. When other spiritual helpers are standing at my shoulder, the child's gaze might fall upon them, following them as they move. It never ceases to amaze me. It is beautiful to observe; they are all knowing.

What happens to these children as they grow? They are here to experience life on Earth, as we all are. We are spiritual souls having a human experience. In time, maybe this lifetime, maybe the next, they too will remember who they are. Maybe they will never forget. That would be quite a thing. When you see that they can see, it is just so beautiful.

We are all born with the knowledge of the Universe inside us but without the ability to communicate it, and then life comes along and buries this knowledge under complex emotional patterning and mental beliefs of ourselves and others. We hide our true selves in order to fit in, to feel love from those around us, to not upset those around us, to feel we belong. It is still there though, our true nature, waiting to rise.

Chapter 6

During the fourth year, we had to sell another car to continue to fund this extraordinary adventure, only this time it was not the one we drove daily. This sale still stings. Of course it was worth it to continue the course, but I really wish we hadn't had to do it. Gary had built a custom wooden garage outside, it even exceeded planning regulations, but we didn't really have any neighbours to complain about it. It had to be built to a specific size to accommodate an old Volkswagen camper that we bought off some friends with the intention of doing it up. I think hubby may have shed a tear for this one, but ever the pragmatist and solid champion of my learning, the old girl was duly sold, sad times. But the accounts department of the college was pacified and kept off our backs a while longer.

The relentless fees continued to rise. At some point, I heard about a charity run by osteopaths called The Osteopathic Foundation. They would lend you a small amount towards your fees if you could go up to the London School of Osteopathy and woo them with your tales of woe. I put on some smart clothes and got on the train for London. What followed was toe curling embarrassing.

I queued up with others hopeful of getting a loan (there was only so much money in the kitty and not everyone would receive help). I put my story to the board. It was like being interviewed before a panel. Answering questions such as "Why are you on this course if you do not have the means to fund it?" "What are you doing to better your chances of affording to finish?" I felt that I could hardly tell them the Universe had decreed it so. That a loud voice in my head had demanded it of me. Maybe I should have. Instead, I discussed how we shopped frugally, had sold all our worldly possessions, how we had taken in a lodger, etc. I was fortunate and grateful that they chose to loan me £3,000, to be paid back on completion of the course. The Universe had my back even if it was toe curling embarrassing. I'm sure it was good for my self-development. I made a vow that day that I would never return there to effectively beg for money. At the time, I felt it was a harsh lesson in being made to feel extraordinarily small.

An only slightly easier beg for money was asking my dad. I had to have a wee drink to pluck up the courage. I do not ask others for help easily. Now, my dad might appear to have no money, his trousers often an odd size and held up by bailing twine, but do not let appearances deceive you. So, after a large tipple, I got on the phone for another begging session. "You can have what's under my mattress," he said, and that was all. Well, there was £1,000 there! So those two scenarios were the sum of financial help for my degree. I paid them both back.

The time came, fees were due, again, and we had to sell the main car, again. We sold the Vauxhall Corsa for a lump sum, and hubby was able to get a wee car on finance with the help of the company he was working for at the time. It was a Citroen C1. Great for whizzing up and down the motorway in, so economical, a very cute but very basic dodgem car. One of my fondest memories is filling the C1 with us two adults, two children, our German Shepherd, our lurcher, and all the paraphernalia for a week's long holiday on the Isle of Wight. How we laughed. Unfortunately, it was not to last.

≂ ★ ≂

I was progressing at the clinic in Hemel Hempstead, I had my own room built just for me. On stepping into the clinic, you would immediately be presented to a rather grand staircase which led upstairs to all the clinic rooms; however, if you went straight ahead, passed the stairs, you would come to the rear entrance. My new room was built under the staircase. It was sectioned off from the staircase with a new door, and the back wall of the room was the back door. I felt honoured to have my own space even if it was a little Harry Potter esc. I was growing as a practitioner; I was able to contribute more to the finances, and that felt good.

It could get quite cosy in my tiny space, and I sometimes felt it was hard to stretch my wings. Not that my wings minded, they were energetic after all and slipped through the walls. It was only my prefrontal cortex, the thinking portion of the left hemisphere of our brain that gives us outline, separation, that kept the room small. When I was working, connecting to others, the border of this reality would blur and soften, everything became one. I have come to learn that this ability arises from utilising the thinking portion of the right hemisphere of our brains. It was as if you could see the individual molecules that made up something, us, an object, a chair. It would become that you could put your hand through a wall, or so it would seem. Reading Jill Bolte Taylors *Whole Brain Living* nearly a decade later gave a lovely framework and physiological grounding to these sensations.

It was in this little room that I had my first real shamanic experience. I was minding my own business in a healing session when suddenly I dropped down into the underworld. I moved along a damp and musky tunnel littered with objects and beings. I walked passed them, they were not what I was looking for. What was I looking for? I did not know, but I knew that when I found it I would know. It turned out to be a tiger. I asked this tiger if it would return with me, to which it agreed. I surfaced fast and upon entering the reality of my room again, I slammed the tiger through the heart space of my patient to which she responded with a large gasp and intake of air. Where she had been dozing, she was now fully present in the room and a little startled to say the least. She was not the only one.

≥ ★ ≤

I wanted to be able to talk to other osteopaths about what I was seeing and feeling. I knew I couldn't be the only one. Help appeared to come from the internet. There was a Facebook group that had been set up called Sacral Musings. How amazing, help and advice at my fingertips. Or so I thought.

I put it out there to my peer group: "What of the spirituality in osteopathy?" "Where was the spirituality in osteopathy?" I got shot down. I got told in no uncertain terms to bring my head back below the parapet. These things were not to be discussed. Especially by a student. I would get my head shot off before I had even begun my career. What a grave disappointment. Osteopathy, after all, is body, mind, *and* spirit. Fortunately, there were a couple of seasoned osteos that privately messaged me and I thank God for them. They kept my spirit up. I think, somewhere along the line, osteopathy may have lost its way in a bid to integrate into the mainstream. This is a shame and too big a discussion for here. For me, the integration of spirit in our holistic healing modality is what sets osteopathy apart.

I was loving the metaphysical aspect of the osteopathy degree even if the course leaders had not realised the extent of that aspect. I loved that I could put hands on a person and call to any part of them and feel that part rise into my hands. I loved being able to tune into different systems of the body whilst still holding absolute awareness that there is only one system, no differentiation and if you dove deep enough you would feel that everything is fluid. The bones are fluid, the muscles, ligaments, and tendons are all fluid. Everything is energy. Everything has a pattern. You do not have to know what the pattern is, only feel that it is incomplete or obstructed. When you engage with the self-healing mechanism of the system, everything rights itself. I began to realise that if I took my brain out of the session and went with intuition, the healing was quite profound. For myself included. Healing is a two-way street.

As I worked on healing myself, other aspects of my life were simultaneously breaking down. My marriage was disintegrating, and I was drinking too much. I had to pause my drinking in order to know that the decisions I was making at this time were the true expression of myself and that my judgement was not clouded by the alcohol.

Chapter 7

Going into the final year, I took the cranial elective. We had to choose if we would be staying on the bachelor pathway or advancing onto the integrated masters pathway that had begun the year prior. I initially started on the master's but thankfully dropped back to the bachelor's. If I was to be performing pure academia, I would have excelled on the masters. Ultimately, I struggled with maintaining the academic and the metaphysical aspects of the course at the same time. It's all well and good saying that I should have focused on the academic and worried about the rest of the stuff after university, but it was just not possible for me. I lived and breathed the spiritual nature of osteopathy. I could not separate it from myself.

My marriage finally ended. We were to become one of the statistics touted at the beginning, although I could not blame the stress of the course. My path had just changed direction. I am predestined to ever follow the energy, the flow. Life is a series of expansions and contractions. There is no right or wrong. Only movement and growth. It is best to grow with the flow. I could not deviate or resist my path, and before I sat my finals, Gary and I had separated. I cannot pretend that it did not put a certain stressful element on the final months of my degree course, but I marched on as always. I still had the unhealthy work ethic of nothing getting in the way of completion, not even a few days to rest and recuperate. I did remain sober through this time of difficult decision making though.

My sobriety did not last, and it was this year that I hit my proverbial rock bottom in relation to alcohol. I had drunk heavily since my teens. I knew I was a high functioning alcoholic. I spent way too much time thinking about where and when I could have my next drink. It didn't feel good anymore. It actually hadn't felt good for a long time, if ever. It could no longer be passed off as hedonism. It was a dependency. I sat on my back doorstep and cried and cried. I cried because I really wanted to stop drinking for good but the dawning realisation that I didn't think I could scared me.

University life continued apace through all of this. With it being the final year, I knew I had to get a handle on my exam nerves. If anyone has ever had to do an objective structured clinical exam (OSCE) or objective structured practical exam (OSPE) you may have an inkling of what I am talking about. In these scenarios I would just fall apart even though I knew the answers; my mind would go blank and all I would be able to squeak out was "I don't know" in answer to any question. The accumulation of everyone else's turmoil was just too much for me at this time and reduced my ability to remain in my own midline. My personal exam nerves and frustrations plus everyone else's was too much. So frustrating.

And like my knight in shining armour, in stepped my friend Max, a hypnotherapist among other wonderful attributes. I can still remember the first time I was hypnotised. I loved the melodic wave of Max's voice as he invited me under. I did not need to imagine my favourite place or picture somewhere safe, as soon as he began to talk, I was off. I journeyed regularly through those sessions, visiting both the upper and lower realms, whilst Max imprinted in my subconscious all that I needed to overcome my exam phobia and ignore everyone else. It really was a masterpiece. By the time I came to my finals, whenever someone asked me a question, I was able to pause, to visit the library in my head, select the relevant book, and give the answer. Absolute magic. Thank you, Max.

I breezed through my finals. I remember sitting outside of the clinic waiting for my turn to enter. A friend knocked on my car window to wish me luck as he walked in for his. I think he was surprised to find me reading *The Way of the Shaman* instead of last-minute osteopathic cramming. The amazing hypnotherapy with my good friend Max saw me very well, and I can still feel the satisfying clonk as my exam patient's sacroiliac joint (SIJ) adjusted perfectly. It remains to this day, along with the neck, my favourite adjustment of all time.

We all passed that day. It was a great day of celebration. We agreed as a class that we would wait for the two students who had decided to press on with the master's pathway so that we could all graduate together. Something happened with those two students, autocratic nonsense, and we never got to have our graduation day with the gowns and mortarboards. This affected me more than I care to admit. I was so proud to have got there. It had seemed like a mission at times. I wanted our journey acknowledged, but it was not to be. Furthermore, the university chose to withhold my degree as I still owed £8,000 in fees from the final year and a bit of year four.

I remained at the clinic in Hemel Hempstead, and as soon as I could, I registered with the Osteopathic Council. I also had a brass sign made up with my name, letters, and registered title. This went some way to alleviate the lack of a graduation ceremony and became the focal point for my success.

I came out with a 2:1 (B+) in the end. Not too shabby considering I had two small children, constant financial pressure, was building a patient list, a marital separation, intermittent alcoholism, and the spiritual realm at my feet.

Chapter 8

In my early twenties, I saw a local tarot reader who told me that my destiny was to be with John. Around this time there may have been a mix up in my thinking and it didn't quite work out as I had hoped. The tarot reader got that wrong then, I thought. Except, after two marriages and two divorces, I finally found my way to my John. She was right after all! Apologies, I take it all back.

I think on a soul level I always knew that I would end up with John. I had known him for some years, an elusive figure in the village. He walked everywhere, and if I happened upon him at the local fireworks or the train station, I would observe him quietly. John, however, remained blissfully unaware.

John and I had a mutual friend in Max (the hypnotherapist I spoke of earlier), and when he was much younger, John had confided in Max that he quite fancied me. Max warned him to steer clear of me at that time. I was riotous, loud, drank too much, took too many drugs, and hung out with a much older group, one of whom was my partner and would go on to become my first husband, Pete. Pete said he didn't want children, and me being young, I thought he would change his mind, but he never did and we split. We have remained friends though.

I always felt myself drawn to John without really knowing why. He was quiet and reserved. At the time, I was 17, loud and obnoxious. I knew deep down he would figure in my future somewhere but now was not the time. We had our own journeys to make first.

Now John was back in the village after a short stint in town. He was living with our good friends Max and Rachael, his wife, who also happened to be my cousin. We had children of the same age and often hung out. My car knew its way to their house without me having to think. Auto pilot driving which was handy if I'd had a few wines in the garden with them, which was often.

I started to see John fairly regularly. Would go up to Max and Rachael's house hoping to catch him when he came in from work. Wanting to see John overlapped with Gary and I splitting up and it led to some high emotions all round. The energy with John was so strong. It just drew me in like a magnet. It could not be ignored. Poor John did not know what hit him. In the face of such intensity, he may have uttered his unsureness. Alas, his fate was sealed as well as mine.

John and I did not officially get together until well after Gary and I split, but there is no doubt that the energetic cords that bind us together were there long before even my first marriage.

It is a bit of a long-standing joke that each husband gets ten years. Well, John currently sits at seven.

Maybe the trick is not to get married.

Maybe there is no trick.

Maybe people come and go from your life with reason and purpose.

Maybe every connection is a chance to learn and heal and grow.

Maybe we should trust that every connection is never mere chance and never a mistake. The Universe knows best after all.

The more of myself I heal, the less inclined I am to marry in the traditional sense. I am bonded with John and do not feel the need for paperwork and all the legalities. When John and I are intimate, a toroidal sphere of energy connects us through our root and crown chakras (energy centres), trumping any need for material proof of our soul love connection.

John has a peaceful, calm energy, and I can sit easily with him in a shared energetic space and not feel discombobulated. Towards the end of our marriage, sleeping in the same bed as Gary, his gentle snoring and soft pfhhhhht out through his lips would, especially if facing toward me, blow my energy field right off me. It was like being on a boat in tumultuous seas all night. I understand now that I was not well grounded, and I dissociated a lot which would have contributed to this overall effect, but at the time it was draining to feel seasick all night. During the day, I would feel fritzy and agitated and never at peace.

In John's energy field, though, I felt peaceful and calm, and this is what my soul cried out for. I was healing myself and I needed peace. John would be my next teacher in this respect. He would show me what it was to slow down, how to be peaceful. A general antithesis to everything I had known. This relationship would take my nervous system from a constant sympathetic state of fight and flight, which I had been in since childhood, to a calmer parasympathetic state of rest where I could further heal myself.

I still get along fabulously with the girls' dad, Gary. He and John also get along very well, bonding over their mutual love of good whiskey. After Gary split with his new partner, he moved back in with us. This was a great situation. Always someone to do the school run, mind the children, or cook dinner. I can thoroughly recommend letting your ex-husband move in with you and your new partner. The girls were ecstatic. A win, win situation and that's how it remained until we shifted to New Zealand.

Part 2

Chapter 9

My patient profiles grew increasingly interesting. I saw fewer sore backs and more diverse cases. Osteopathy has a reputation for being good with sore backs. This came about after a piece of research back in the nineties. A randomised controlled trial that verified that osteopaths had positive results with nonspecific low back pain. This was the bane of my early osteopathic life but only until the energy had settled and I began to attract the kind of patients that would benefit from my particular set of skills.

Osteopathy is fantastically holistic. It looks at the whole person, never one part in isolation. One person's low back pain may be, and often is, entirely different to another's. And just to throw in a bag of tangents, health and well-being is much more than the physical aspect of the person and extends far beyond the tissue causing symptoms of the physical system. If I had to see physical bad backs in isolation of everything else, I might die of boredom. Well, not really. There is beauty in the mundane after all. Plus, I am always eternally grateful to pay my rent.

In grateful actuality, I saw a lot of energetically dysfunctional cases and remain blissfully fortunate for the sight and depth of feeling gifted to me. Patients might not have come to me realising this was their issue, but this is what would often show up.

A lady presented to me, only in her thirties; she had children; she was stressed, discombobulated; and found intercourse uncomfortable. She felt she was lacking connection. She had gone into hospital for a basic operation, and they had ended up performing a full hysterectomy without her prior knowledge or consent, ultimately leading to premature menopause. Her system was in shock, and she had not integrated the lack of a uterus and cervix into her energetic make up. There was a strong disconnect there. After integrating her surgery into her emotional, mental, and spiritual fields, she regained her zest for life, reconnected to those around her, got her sex life back, and generally felt much better.

A young married man presented with a withered right leg which caused him to limp. It had been this way for decades. Putting hands on, I could feel that his right leg was not connected to his energy fields. When questioned further as to what may have caused this, he remembered a moped accident in India decades previously where he had crashed and the moped had landed and trapped his right leg. Once we reconnected the leg, he was able to build strength back in the limb. Sensation came back to the limb, and when I last saw him, he was enjoying attending the gym and working to equalize the strength and build of his legs.

A post-menopausal lady attended for long standing low back pain. By putting hands on, we were immediately transported to her time in utero. When born, she had not fully extended her system. She was still energetically in the foetal position. Her system was desperate to uncurl, she just needed a little impetus to achieve this.

She was able to uncurl to full extension. Most of her discomfort resolved immediately.

In these incidents, it did not take long at all for improvements. Huge benefits were felt instantly and more so with subsequent follow-ups. I was, and still am, blown away by the healing capacity of our systems if we are just able to look beyond the physical self.

We are also grossly affected by what we do to ourselves, do to others, or have done to us by others. Abuse, addiction, medical procedures, the environment around us, our food, what we do day in day out. All these things affect our physical body, our emotional body, our mental body, and our spiritual body.

In the case of medical procedures, especially noted with injections, a disconnect to the receiving limb via the energy field can be felt. The energetic patterns of the limb need to be run in order to reconnect it to the whole field. Now, this type of shock can be felt and can affect us anywhere in our system, but for the sake of you reading this, I shall refer to the thoracic diaphragm as it is often affected in most traumatic patterns and most people will be familiar with it.

The thoracic diaphragm, which hopefully many of us *are* familiar with, attaches at the front of your sternum at the lowest palpable (felt) bony prominence of the xiphoid process, all around the lower ribs and at the level of T12, the last spinous process of the thoracic spine before it becomes the lumbar spine.

The shock of any procedure, especially if unaware it is coming, can affect the thoracic diaphragm, our main muscle of secondary respiration, breathing.

Our thoracic cage, made up of our ribs which protect our lungs, can tighten and shorten, thus reducing lung capacity, and we can become more prone to coughs and colds and chest infections. If our thoracic cage reduces and tightens, it leaves less space for the fluids of the head to drain into the thoracic cage to get to where it needs to go to be recycled or expelled. This can lead to congestion causing tension and headaches, ear infections, tooth infections, and so on.

Physical shock is not the only shock we can experience. Emotional shock can also lead to dysfunctional patterns of the thoracic diaphragm. This can lead to shock held in the system. Emotional cysts, bubbles of energy of an emotional nature that we are unable to deal with presently bundled up neatly and left in the system until such a time as we are ready to revisit it, are often felt at the level of the thoracic diaphragm. This is our horizontal midline and passes through the solar plexus, the third main centre of our energetic system known as the chakra system, often associated with family.

Who of us can lay claim to a non-dysfunctional family? Certainly not me and the shock of a revelation in my youth left me with a huge emotional cyst that I carried with me, was aware of, was frustrated by and then eventually made peace with, that sat at my solar plexus for many, many years. It left when the time was right. Expelled in quite a spectacular and forceful manner, more of which I'll discuss later.

In patients, however, this shock often presents as heartburn, acid reflux, digestive trouble, irritable bowel syndrome and such. For myself, I often had mucus in my stools, a strong sign of a system under pressure but something I had experienced for so long but never really gave any consideration to. My bladder, where fear and fright reside, had been overactive since the revelation. Along with the inability to draw a proper breath, grief sat on my lungs. My system had not worked at its optimum for many years. The physical pump mechanism of the diaphragm was not clearing my system effectively. In my youth I suffered recurrent tonsillitis but instead of dealing with the underlying cause and returning efficiency to my system, I had my tonsils removed when I was 15.

I would often wish I still had my tonsils but understand that it was a lack of knowledge. Hell, I had not even heard of any kind of bodywork in my youth, and it was not something anyone in my family engaged with. I was non-blissfully unaware that it existed and that there was another way.

We can become embroiled with these traumatic patterns; we tell ourselves untruths. Unhealthy mental thought patterns and processes can dominate our lives. The attitudes and beliefs of others that imprint on us that are not actually the truth of who we are. These mental thought patterns can lead to extreme coping mechanisms such as addiction, withdrawal, procrastination, compensation by way of over working, etc. In my case it was alcoholism.

I see patients that have dissociated from themselves because something so terrible has happened to them which has left them unable to remain in themselves. Their energy fields can become distorted. The thread which emanates from the area of the solar plexus and connects us to the placenta of the Universe, to which we are all connected, can become frayed with total disconnect presumably resulting in death.

Not having had the privilege of being present at the time of someone's passing, I cannot confirm or deny my presumption, but I can say for certainty that when I see a connection to the Universe in a less-than-desirable condition. The person will no doubt be having issues across all fields: physical, emotional, mental, and spiritual. We can tune into these fields, and I am fortunate to be able to do this. During treatment, this arises organically; I do not seek to go there intentionally.

Often when physical issues resolve, I will see the impact upon the other fields. The emotional body will clear through, and this has a sensation of water over pebbles along the vertical midline the width of the body. Then often the mental body will clear, and I see this as two energy lines running parallel to the physical body, emanating from the top of the head, the crown, and returning via the root of our body, the base of our spine, our pelvic floor. This sends a clearance up the spine, back out through the crown, along the parallel energy lines and back up the base and so on. Once cleared through the mental body, the system sends a shock wave, a sonic boom, in all directions from the vertical and horizontal midlines. The healing that has taken place within you reverberates throughout the Universe via your spiritual body. Your connection to the Universe is strengthened.

When you think that you are just one person and that what you do will not make a difference, trust me, it does. Negatively and positively, whatever we do affects the whole. It really is a case of working on yourself to heal the world. We all have the task of transitioning from our personal darkness and into our own light. It is the hardest work of all, and each of us has the same job in this respect.

Chapter 10

I had felt that something was fundamentally missing for me in osteopathy, from my own osteopathic practice and application, since graduating. I felt that women were being short-changed. I felt, *knew*, I could do more for them across a variety of issues but needed more structure to this area of work.

Ladies were being told that a multitude of their female related issues were the natural occurrences of being female and having all the experiences that females entail and that not much could be done for them. I drew on my personal birthing experiences and issues with secondary infertility, and my interest in pelvic work accelerated.

My firstborn, Edie, was born via emergency caesarean section five weeks shy of her due date. Knowing what I know now, this birth would have been very different. But I was young and scared, and fear driven situations and solutions are quite prevalent on the obstetric ward. It was thought that I was leaking amniotic fluid and that I had Group B strep present in my vagina, and so I was induced. Group B strep is one of the many bacteria that normally live in our bodies which usually cause no harm.

For the induction, oxytocin was intravenously administered to bring about labour. The contractions came hard and fast, no let-up in between with limited dilation. I barely had time to draw breath before my body was wracked by the next intense artificial contraction. Due to not dilating quickly enough in my allotted time slot, I was deemed having failed to progress, so was whipped in for an emergency C-section. It is not uncommon for birthing to end in C-section once induced and frequently a cascade of dysfunction will follow induction.

In my first birthing experience, I was physically kept from Edie as she was in the special care baby unit (SCBU), and I staggered around the hospital looking and crying out for her, clutching my C-section wound. No one stopped to help me or ask what I was doing. I was still under the effects of anaesthesia and was confused. I found Edie eventually and refused to be parted from her. I could not breastfeed initially as they also thought she may have meningitis, so she was hooked up to intravenous antibiotics. Such a lot for her young body. I sat desolate, attached to the mechanical breast pump so that my baby might have all the benefits of the colostrum. I managed to produce so much colostrum that I added greatly to the stocks in the SCBU so that other babies could also be fed this very beneficial first milk.

All I wanted was to take my baby home, but we were kept in for weeks, sleeping in a little room near Edie. Even when the time came for Edie to be discharged, we were not allowed to take her as we had not registered with a new doctor in the town we had recently moved to even though my own doctor that I had for most of my life was only 6 miles (10km) down the road and whom I hadn't intended on changing. Bureaucratic nonsense made a stressful period even more so.

My second born, Lily, was conceived very quickly after Edie. My thinking at the time was that if I didn't do it again swiftly, such was the trauma of Edie's birth, I would never do it again. Edie was born in October and Lily was conceived in the following February. The consensus was that I would have another C-section as it was dangerous to give birth vaginally so soon after the C-section. I did not want another C-section and was determined to have a vaginal birth. The medical fraternity put their foot down in terms of a home birth, and I gave birth in hospital vaginally with the help (?) of an epidural, front to back episiotomy (cut from vagina to anus with subsequent deep stitching), and a ventouse to suction Lily out.

With Lily, I was physiologically kept from her, distanced by drugs and lack of feeling. I went into labour naturally but was made to stop pushing after only a short time due to the obstetrician's fear of my prior C-section scar erupting. Once the epidural was administered, I lost all control over the birth, could no longer feel myself pushing, and medical intervention took over. I was so out of it on the drugs that when Lily was born and they asked if I would like to hold her, I requested some toast and a cup of tea instead. This haunts me to this day, and I can only hope that Lily did not feel the effects of this dismissal and knows that I love her with all my heart and it was not my intention for the birth to go this way.

Of course, in both cases, I was eternally grateful my babies were here with me, but I knew there would be a long path of healing and learning to come from these two birthing stories which were impacted by fear, not wholly of my own making.

Now, John and I had been trying for a baby for nearly a year with no success. I knew this was not an issue for me considering my history. Although I had experienced quite a few miscarriages, most likely due at the time to my alcohol addiction and recreational drug use and my emotional and mental wellbeing, I had eventually borne two daughters with Gary before my osteopathic study and own healing journey commenced.

John and I wanted a baby together. John was getting on a bit, and I suppose I was, too. Although, I believe the term "geriatric mother" is offensive and not applicable in most cases. If you are fit and well, have a passion for life and are still ovulating, it would seem nature deems you fit enough to be a parent. Drop the geriatric bit please. I also trusted that we would conceive.

One morning I had been upset at this predicament we found ourselves in. Sitting on our back doorstep crying, I looked up as a white pheasant crossed our front garden. I had not seen one before, and I haven't seen one since. I need not worry myself further, I told myself. A symbol of fertility so obviously given. Thank you, Universe.

I have long interpreted the messages from Spirit that come via animals. If you are going through something, pay attention to any strange animal occurrences. An animal you might not normally see in everyday life, an animal out of its normal setting, an animal that approaches you, makes eye contact with you. If something strikes you as unusual or peaks your interest, it is easy to look up the spiritual meaning of said animal, and you will most likely take useful insights or comfort from your animal interaction.

After the visit of the white pheasant and after some time trying, we purchased a home sperm test for John from Amazon. The results were not encouraging. On the back of this, we booked him in for testing through the GP. Almost zero sperm count and what was there were a funny shape and didn't move. Well, as an osteopath, I thought about what could be done for John and what John could do to help himself.

Whilst waiting for a follow up appointment with the GP, we adjusted John's diet. We googled what vitamins and nutrients he needed to up his man game and from what food he could derive these. He drank super smoothies every morning. Stopped smoking. Stopped his occasional whiskey. I cleared the congestion in his pelvis. Got everything moving. I tracked my fertility and still have the beautiful graph from our month of conception.

We took the Australian view of conception. Plaster as much sperm as possible over the cervix as often as possible. The Brits have a more conservative view, especially when you have a low sperm count. You must give it your best shot and then conserve your energy whilst you build up your reserves again. My impatience and gut instinct did not allow for this method. Poor John. I didn't make him perform every night, but through my fertile phase, if we did not feel like it, we simply used syringes – also purchased from Amazon. I think it is entirely possible that Walker was conceived using this method, with my legs up the wall watching "Strictly Come Dancing".

In time, we attended a follow up appointment to discuss the outcome of John's tests. Here they told us he would never be able to father children. They cupped his testicles and told him it was because he had had mumps when he was younger. We were told that in vitro fertilization (IVF) would not be enough for us and that we would have to use intracytoplasmic sperm injection (ICSI) as well. When I questioned our ability to naturally conceive, we were told that if we were to conceive naturally (very low chance) that there would be a strong possibility that our child would have a defect or deformity. It was probably for this reason that we sat quietly and did not inform the doctor that I was already pregnant.

Walker's pregnancy and birth went smoothly. I was older now, knew more, had more confidence in myself and the process. Even when they wanted to induce me because I had gone over forty-two weeks, I held fast. I gave birth at home as I wished, leaving John asleep until around 3am whilst I happily bounced on my ball. The midwife came around 6am and Walker was born shortly after. I was left mostly to my own devices. I loved it. He would have been birthed on all fours except right at the end the midwife was unsure of where the baby's head was and what she was feeling so turned me over. Walker was born face first. The midwife was shocked. In her twenty years of home birth, she had never birthed a face first. She said he should have been a C-section. Erm, no thanks, we were both quite happy at home.

He latched in a funny position initially as his neck had overextended with the face first delivery and he had swelling to the face. The midwife wanted us to go to the hospital.

"Do not worry," I said. "By tomorrow he will be right as rain."

I treated him and by the next day all was well. When I say treated, I joined with him, we became one, and he, so recently born to this world, holder of all universal knowledge, happily unwound his birthing strain patterns, swiftly and peacefully. By the next morning he was latching beautifully, head and neck in good position, swelling all but gone and head shaping nicely. Being an osteopath is awesome. The Universe is awesome.

We celebrated with champagne, expertly timed throughout breastfeeding so as not to affect the baby. As much as I reassured myself that drinking whilst breastfeeding in this way would not affect the baby, it is not something I would dream of advocating. Thankfully, all my children seem to have come through relatively unscathed by my alcohol addiction. Thank the Universe.

His birthing experience went a long way to alleviate the trauma of my first two, and although his ginger hair was a beautiful shock, he has no known defects to date.

I, on the other hand, through my trials and tribulations trying to conceive and give birth naturally, encountered infertility, miscarriages, birth trauma, C-section, episiotomy, tearing, stitching, urinary incontinence, haemorrhoids, pain during pregnancy, pain during intercourse, diastasis recti (separation of abdominal muscles), and subsequently a weak core and pelvic floor. No more trampolining for me. Hang on a minute …

And right there I found what was missing for me. I wanted to help women like me, I wanted to empower them. I wanted them to know they had options and there were solutions. That we didn't have to put up with painful intercourse, that there were things we could do for women and men to help our quest to conceive. That we do not have to have an eternally leaky bladder. I've lost count of the number of women that have confided in me that they have had incontinence (rectal or bladder) or that intercourse was so painful since the birth of their children they had given up having it all together, and sometimes that was decades ago. It was either not talked about or when it was, it was dismissed as normal after certain experiences. Holy moly.

The drive to help myself and other women like me, set me off on the next part of my osteopathic odyssey. Primarily it was all about women's pelvic health, but it has extended to cover men's pelvic health. It takes two to tango after all.

Chapter 11

When Walker was about 6 months old, John fell gravely ill. Walker still slept with us, and John would keep us awake at night so was relegated to the put-up bed in the front room to recuperate. We thought he had the flu, but instead of rallying, he continued to get worse. I had to go to work one morning but asked Gary to run him to the doctors. I should have taken him the night before, but I had been drinking and could not drive, it was just the flu after all.

Instead of seeing the doctor, he was swiftly taken to hospital. His temperature was sky high, in the 40s. Nothing they gave him would bring it down. They tried many different intravenous antibiotics. We were told to prepare for the worst if it could not be brought down.

We were panic stricken; John was delirious. I was spending all my time at the hospital with a small baby – not ideal. John had no family locally, so I phoned his most reliable brother and he came down from up north, nearly a three hour drive away. I was so grateful for his help. He stayed with John when I had to take some time out. Gary looked after the girls.

The complete insanity and speed at which John became very poorly, combined with lack of sleep and stress that our lives could be irrevocably changed, knocked me right out of my midline. It is hard to remain grounded and transparent, objective even, when the sick person in front of you is one of your own.

A new nurse came on shift after a couple of days and suggested he could have Legionnaires' disease. As it turned out, he did. Legionnaires' disease is a water borne bacterial infection resulting in a very serious type of pneumonia. It is a notifiable disease in the UK, and we had to trace and report John's whereabouts for the last two weeks prior to becoming ill. The source could not be found and it was presumed that he may have caught it by inhaling the legionella bacteria from an air vent as he walked around London. He would walk from Euston Station to his workplace in Central London most days, a twenty-minute stroll. Just a random occurrence.

His temperature still raged, even with the right medication, and he was bonkers for quite some time. Hallucinating that he was in the Scottish or Welsh highlands and frequently trying to escape, albeit in his very polite, English way. Middle of the night escapades: "Excuse me nurse, might you just unlock the door for me so I may return home." They said he was the politest, most persistent patient they had ever had.

It was a nerve-wracking time, considering that I may lose my love, the father of my small boy, this early in our journey together. John would frequently try to remove his antibiotic intravenous line whilst shouting claims of being poisoned. For someone who rarely if ever took any medications I am sure this is exactly how his system felt, and I struggled with the limited mainstream medical view on treatment and lack of acceptance that other methods or modalities could possibly help John recover. I was eternally grateful of course that John was alive, and once the immediate threat of death had passed, set about rejuvenating him.

I asked that my colleague and good friend Sydommne might come in to administer homeopathic medicine, but with their limited knowledge of homeopathy and how it worked the doctors were loath to let her in. So we smuggled her in instead. The change in John as the homeopathic medicine started was obvious. He calmed down; his temperature came down. He began to recognise that he was not in fact in the mountains but in Aylesbury General Hospital. John was coming back to us.

He developed an obsession with marmalade toast having never previously had a penchant for it. It is pretty much all he would eat once on his way to recovery in the hospital, so some credit must also go to the marmalade and the nurses that continued to supply him. His great love for it continues to this day, a reminder of this time.

The support we received from Sydommne though was unwavering, and I believe with her help, John began to turn a corner. I was deeply saddened to learn only five years later that she had passed away. A beautiful soul. So much gratitude for her kindness.

I reflected on Johns treatment for a long time afterwards. How quickly you can lose your midline in times of huge stress. I know if it were to happen again I would call on my natural health colleagues sooner, favouring a multidisciplinary approach to health.

There was a strong possibility that John would be left with long term fatigue, and I wanted to combat this early on and get his system fired up and working again. A "use it or lose it" approach. What we were not so aware of was the chance of memory and concentration issues, of possible neurological and muscular issues.

When he was well enough to leave the hospital a long week later, it was the depth of winter. To aid him in his recovery, I took him to the Welsh Highlands, the mountains that he loves so much, and had him push his small son's mountain buggy around the snowy hills. No better way to recover from a potentially life-threatening lung disease than a little exertion, breathing fresh mountain air.

John had always had a very calm temperament. After the recovery from the disease, however, he would became quite fritzy in situations where there was too much stimulation. Too much sensory input and the children could easily overload him. I was nervous that this new state would prevail, and I fear I may have added to his overload in my bid to have him well again.

Although I sensed that he would ultimately be well, I could not allow myself to rest easy in this knowing. I almost felt that if I were to relax and accept that all would be well that I would somehow jinx it and the opposite would happen. I felt that on some level I needed to stress about it. It was a stressful situation after all.

John also found that his concentration lapsed. That he could not cope with stressful situations. John was a model maker, a prototype engineer for a design company. His job was stressful, running on tight budgets and project realisation timelines. He was well known for his ability to pull an all-nighter to meet deadlines. He had worked for the same company for over twenty years. His job was wonderful in waiting for him to return, which he probably did way too soon.

He found that he could no longer easily maintain working in this environment. His hands shook when he tried to concentrate on intricate models, and he felt as if his head would explode if too much was asked of him. He was deeply worried that he would not be able to continue. His hands were his livelihood and his creative joy.

John is better now but no longer has a desire to work in such a pressured environment; this could be a natural progression – he is nearing retirement age. He still has memory lapses but these could be attributed to the fact that he does not fully integrate what I am saying to him a lot of the time, in one ear and out the other. His head nears explosion at times, but so does mine, living with teenagers can be mind-blowing. And he is much windier! John attributes this to the multitude of antibiotics he took, but I think it may also be because he eats actual food now, his system no longer running solely on caffeine and nicotine.

John and I were not together for a substantial period prior to his illness so it's hard to know if these are natural progressions for him or a lasting result of being very unwell. I can't remember how he was prior, only that he was always an incredibly calm man. What does it matter though? There is only now, and ultimately it's all about the lessons. What we take from these experiences and how we grow as the spiritual human beings we are. I cannot speak for John directly, but at a grass root level, I would guess his lesson involved slowing down and taking more care of himself. Maybe he did not notice the smaller signs, so the Universe sent him a big one. A big healing crisis as a transition to higher planes.

Me? I should not have been drinking. Would I have realised how poorly John was if I had not been drinking that evening? Drinking made me selfish. I was constantly stressed about work, being financially stable, being there for the children. The classic work/life balance conundrum. Always on the go, seeking respite in alcohol. I also needed to prioritise what was important in my life. The drinking needed to stop. Lessons everywhere. Everything exactly as it should be.

Chapter 12

When I got together with John, I asked him if he could live anywhere in the world, where would it be? He replied that he loved the UK but would consider one other country: New Zealand. Well, happy days! Me too! I was just waiting to qualify and then I would make my move. Somehow.

I have always felt a very strong pull to New Zealand. Since my teens, even though I had never visited, I just knew I would end up there. You know that feeling that sits so comfortably with you that you are so sure, in no uncertain terms that whatever this is, it is just going to come to fruition. You may not know exactly how you are going to get from A to B, but you just trust that you are.

Well, there's nothing like a near death experience to set your priorities in order. It was time to get the ball rolling. The devil is in the detail though.

Due to my deep-seated knowledge that I would one day live there, I had already spent decades following Immigration New Zealand and all the changes they had made over the years to allow people to move, work, and live in New Zealand. I had watched the points threshold for a skilled migrant residency visa move from 100 to

120, then to 140, and then to 160, which was where it stood when I wanted to apply.

With the skilled migrant residency visa, you accrued points for things like your age, the younger you were the more you were worth. Conversely you also score points for your work experience in your area of skilled expertise. I couldn't move straight after qualifying as I did not score enough points. Your points went up the more years work experience you had, *but* they also went down the older you got. Having started osteopathy as a mature student, time was not on my side. By now, I had been qualified and working long enough to claim the lowest number of work experience points, but I had crept up into the 40–45 age bracket, so my age points were decreasing.

For many years prior and whilst I was studying, osteopathy had been on the most wanted list, so would have given me further big bonus points, but just as I graduated, they took it off. Having graduated with a degree also scored me points. The higher your level of education, the more points you scored. With osteopathy now off the most wanted list, gaining entry would be far harder. I would need a job offer to obtain the necessary points. And not just any job offer.

A job offer from a clinic in Auckland would not score me enough points, but as this is where the vast majority of New Zealanders live and also where a large portion of the 550 registered osteopaths in New Zealand live it also meant it was the area with most job vacancies. To put it in perspective, New Zealand has a population of approximately 5 million and approximately 1.6 million live in Auckland with the rest spread out across the country which comprises of two islands of similar size. The North and the South Islands. The North Island, which is where Auckland is situated, has a population of approximately 4 million, whilst the South Island, with less habitable space, has the remaining 1 million. New Zealand has a total land mass similar to the UK, which has a population of approximately 67 million, and ten times the number of osteopaths.

I could totally understand New Zealand wanting to further populate the rest of the country beyond Auckland and the steps they implemented to make this so, but I bemoaned the hurdles I faced in getting to where I knew I needed to be.

Finding a job offer outside of Auckland was going to be tricky, but that is what I needed to do to gain the final 30 points to take me to exactly the 160-point threshold. I knew the Universe had my back. I had seen New Zealand in my future for so long but sometimes the rational mind does boggle at exactly how these things will eventuate.

I was still looking to further my education by way of women's health. I was having real trouble finding anything of osteopathic continued professional development (CPD) that was resonating with me, and I was strongly considering doing a midwifery degree. Luckily, at the eleventh hour (because doing another degree would be insanity), I stumbled upon the Molinari Institute for Health who ran a new two-year postgraduate diploma in women's health especially for osteopaths.

This was the first postgraduate diploma of its kind worldwide for osteopaths. Hallelujah. I just had to get accepted. They only took approximately 30 people every two years, and I was applying for the second ever cohort that they had run. To spread the knowledge worldwide, they looked to take people from all corners of the world so that they could return to their home countries with this knowledge and hopefully inspire and teach others. I sent off my application and kept everything crossed.

Deep down, in that place of all knowing, I knew I would be accepted ... and I was. I had realised that I would not be able to apply to move to New Zealand just yet because they had removed osteopathy from the most wanted list. I would have to get a job offer to be in with any chance. I couldn't yet apply for a job because I had been accepted on my two-year postgraduate diploma, and I knew I wanted to complete that first.

For some crazy reason I thought that I would apply for Australia as osteopaths were still on their most wanted list, and I could gain enough points without a job offer. Australia was never the goal. Just a stepping stone to New Zealand as they have lovely reciprocal living arrangements. I thought I would have the application bubbling away in the background whilst I studied again, and on completion of my postgraduate diploma, we could all step gaily onto a plane and make our giant leap to the South Pacific.

Getting into Australia was shaping up to be quite difficult too, though. I had enough points, bolstered by the fact I had taken an English exam. I had to study for it too. Being an English speaker in these tests can be a detriment sometimes. As we understand, we tend not to focus on taking it all in and in a timed scenario, this can be a disadvantage. Sorry, what did you say? I wasn't listening properly. I sat the IELTS English language test and thankfully scored "Superior English", much to John's surprise, and that got me twenty further points. I always say "me" in these situations because John, although top of his tree in his profession in the UK, was deemed too old, and without having a degree, not worthy of any contributing points whatsoever for either Australia or New Zealand. He and the children would be coming on my coat tails.

You know what I did need though for my visa application ...

my bloody osteopathic degree. So much had happened in the time that had passed since 2015. Where was it? I could not believe that I couldn't find it. I have kept all certificates from secondary school up, even my MENSA challenge one which showed I was a wee genius, and my Chelsea Flower Show exhibit silver medal – proud grin. I phoned up the university to see if they could send me a copy.

It was during this call that I learnt it wasn't that I had lost my degree, it was because I still hadn't cleared my student debt, and they were holding it to ransom. I had been steadily paying off my debt and had forgotten about my degree certificate completely. I had obviously been able to sign up with the Osteopathic Council in the UK after our final exams and thought no more of it. Now, I desperately needed my degree transcript for immigration and still owed the university about £4,000.

I hadn't previously considered getting an actual big girl loan. After a misspent youth and time running from debt collectors, I was well and truly put off any form of credit. And I thought I wouldn't be eligible anyway. Well, it turned out I was wrong. Spurred on by my sister, I looked at my profile on a credit database and it appeared that time spent behaving oneself and a couple of marriages later I was once again credit worthy. An actual bona-fide "adult". I took out a loan, thank you Tesco supermarket. I even got a good rate due to having a Clubcard, the supermarket reward scheme. I paid off the remainder of my student debt, and lo and behold, a shiny degree promptly arrived in the post.

I use the term "adult" loosely as I had a little reversion to my youth around this time. Studying osteopathy came with some spoken and some largely unspoken rules around how you should look, and it became glaringly obvious that it came down to how some of the lecturers perceived your appearance. For example, no heavy makeup, no long nails (understandable, patient comfort), no tattoos on display, no piercings other than basic earrings, no coloured hair beyond natural looking, and no outrageous hairstyles. I could understand the need for a uniform clinic clothing and corridor creeper shoe combo, but it felt quite stuffy and outdated to be allowed zero self-expression in terms of one's appearance.

It became quite uncomfortable when one tutor took an open dislike to one student's hairstyle, a perfectly reasonable and professional style in my opinion. It was quite the standoff from which the mature student did not back down. He rightly kept his hairstyle. Maybe the lecturer had taken a dislike to the student and took it out on his hair. Who knows. The beautician/massage therapist dropped out. You get the picture: there were certain standards to be upheld. I was at one point ridiculed for reading The Sun newspaper, a low rent tabloid, during a break. Lin, the clinic manager had left it lying around, and as it was the tabloid of my youth, I had no hesitation in picking it up. I rarely read any tabloid these days, but the ribbing I received further compounded the sense that this was not a working-class environment.

Due to this, I think I suffered from repressed expression. And much to the surprise of our young daughters who were instructed to find every earring or piece of jewellery in the house, I proceeded to re-pierce every available (closed) hole on my body. Some of these had lain unadorned for fifteen years or more, including my nose and tongue which took some persuasion. It was quite uncomfortable to sleep on my ears for some time after this, and I would sleep with a donut pillow. I also began adding to my tattoo collection, which I had largely kept hidden at university, and they began to peep out from under my clinic clothes. I'm quite sure my patients hardly noticed; they were only concerned as to whether I could alleviate their discomfort. But it all felt rather freeing for me, regaining my individual identity. My core, my deep-seated sense of self expanding with the Universe.

I also started the process for registration ($1,750 AUD) as an osteopath in Australia. It would require me to send all my paperwork from the UK, and once satisfied that I was a bona fide UK trained and registered osteopath, I could sit the Australian Osteopathic Accreditation Council (AOAC) open book exam, which I duly did and passed and got the certificate for. Now I needed to go to Australia and complete my registration by way of six months supervised work. I just needed to get selected.

Alas, I did not get picked out of the magical hat for Australia. In retrospect, phew. What a complete roundabout way of trying to get to where you needed to go. It would have been so much easier on myself and those around me to have just sat patiently and trusted the process. The human me always needs a "just in case" scenario. If the Universe doesn't show up for me, I've got this option in my pocket.

If I had really, deep down, wanted to get pulled out of the Australian hat quicker, I could have applied for some jobs; I was just keeping (unnecessarily) busy. It kept me motivated and focused, albeit quite expensively. It also kept me engaged in the visa process. I felt I was doing something, being proactive. I'm not good at having to sit and be patient. Lots of lessons to be learned here. I did get good practice at the visa application, form filling, and necessary requirements, so when the time came for NZ, it was less of a shock. Don't misunderstand me though, the New Zealand visa process was still a massive shocker.

Chapter 13

A couple of years after graduating and after time spent nursing Walker on maternity leave, I moved into refurbished premises in my hometown of Tring. I had dearly loved my time at the clinic in Hemel Hempstead, the opportunity and support they had given me to begin work prior to my actual osteo qualification was incredible, but I could feel the time was right for a change. I wanted my own space on my own terms, and I wanted to be closer to home.

My new space, in a beautifully renovated silk mill that was a prominent feature of my childhood, was huge to make up for the time spent in the Harry Potter staircase room. It was approximately fifteen times bigger than my space in Hemel Hempstead. My energy could fill it though. Expansion! Unfortunately, I was paying by the square foot. Not being particularly business minded though, I did not care.

In September of 2017, I also began my two-year Women's Health Diploma which would see me regularly getting the train or driving the other way around the M25 to South London. Boy, do I dislike the M25. Whenever I think of it from New Zealand, if I try to imagine arriving at Heathrow and having to drive on it, it gives me the heebie jeebies, and I can once again feel the crushing weight of humanity upon my soul.

The pressure of studying is akin to childbirth: so very painful at the time that we vow never to do it again, and then time sugar coats our memories and suddenly it looks enticing again. Cray cray as our daughters would say. Anyway, aside from the logistics, financial pressure once again (approximately £4,000 per year) and the sheer insanity of life, the women's health course was a marvellous revelation.

Once again, the first day was pivotal for understanding what lay ahead. It was revealed to us that some members of the cohort had expressed concerns that men were on the course. It is my understanding that maybe the first cohort, for whatever reason, comprised of females only. Women only on a women's health course kind of jazz. In all honesty, the idea that men might be on the course had not crossed my mind, only because it didn't bother or concern me. I was not known to be shy and retiring, although interestingly, during times of sobriety, I tend to resonate more as an introvert. That notwithstanding, having children predisposed the loss of my modesty and whatever was left got knocked out during my osteopathic degree.

Some ladies though, rightly or wrongly, were concerned. To balance these fears, the principal would include a module covering male pelvic health. The men would not escape the trials and tribulations of practising internal techniques on one another. That's right, osteopaths practice on one another! Seems logical right. Well, I thought so. I have come to realise though that what we encountered on that course was very privileged. Not only to be in actual contact with the very thing which formed the basis of our learning but for the sheer fact that all of us in that room consented for the others to enter those deep places of our souls. It is still, to this day, an enormous privilege and honour to be able to do what we do.

Time has taught me that not everyone trains this way. Of conversations that I am privy to, it became clear that some physios practice on simulated models. Cue strange visions of weird, animated, latex, bucking bronco style pelvic models. And when I had the audacity to ask a women's health GP if they practised on each other, you could have picked her chin up off the floor. Heaven forbid! Of course not. They write the theory and practice on the public.

You can see why I quite rightly think that osteopathy is the *very best* of professions, and I am eternally grateful that we had the opportunity to learn from each other in this way. Even if some days, I could quite happily have throttled the next person that touched my cervix. And as it turned out, having men in the class was a bonus! After all, we all wanted to palpate a prostate. Alas, the ratio of women to men was not in their favour. But I give them their due, I never once heard them complain.

The women's health course trundled on, and I was enjoying putting my new-found knowledge and skills to good use in clinic. Pain during intercourse, prolapse, incontinence, tampons that shot out as soon as you put them in? Yes, yes, yes, happy to help. That's not to say I didn't make some faux pax. Sometimes I was still too shy to look directly and intently at the vagina in question and I can still feel my cheeks flush as one lady commented, "Wrong hole." Oops, my bad.

I also have a certain propensity to make ladies laugh during these examinations, which is counter-intuitive as the vagina can be quite powerful and I get laughed out. I also learned very early on to make sure that I give a full and robust explanation of what the examination and treatment of this area looks like and what may occur during. It is reassuring for the patient and sets my focus well. This was after contacting one lady's pelvic fascia whilst chatting away, and it reacted with such force that it spun my examining arm nearly a full 360 degrees, judo pinning me to the examination couch. How we laughed.

We were very fortunate through the course to have the opportunity to attend a dissection in Nice, France. It would seem there was rather less red tape than the UK, and we were able to commence with the dissection the day after the dear lady's death. A much fresher, more pliable cadaver. My instinct was to hold the lady's hand during the dissection and at times found myself doing so. The surgeon opened the abdomen and pelvis for us. The smell took some acclimatising to. There is nothing quite like seeing it in the flesh so to speak. Quite different yet strangely reminiscent of the frog dissection we undertook in secondary school. We looked, touched, and held all the viscera of the abdomen and pelvis. As an aside, we got to see how cancer looks in the body: like chalk. Like your organ turned to dust. Quite alarming.

After the surgeon had stitched the cadaver back up, he gave permission for us to dissect the upper leg. Giving us the opportunity to see the soft tissue layers and bony components in real time. This relatively short experience in France did more for my comprehension and understanding of the physical body than all my graduate anatomy classes combined. I have huge gratitude to that lady for gifting us that opportunity, and it is a shame that graduates in the UK no longer get to attend a dissection as part of their degree.

My alcohol consumption peaked again around this time, and once again, I took a long sabbatical from consuming. It would turn out to be my longest sabbatical ever, over two years. In the five years leading up to this time, it was not unusual for me to stop drinking for sustained periods of time. Once I even did a year. If I didn't drink, I didn't smoke. Winning. But I always fell off the wagon. Telling myself I could handle it. I would just drink socially. That I could stop when I wanted. Except I couldn't.

I remember this time specifically because, as it was an educational jolly to Nice, John and I doubled it up as a romantic long weekend away. Oh, the struggle! Sun, sea, coffee shops, bars, the French drinking and smoking all over the place. The struggle was real. This fortunately was counterbalanced rather nicely by the fact that we had an incredible Air BnB in the old part of town. It was a huge, elegant penthouse with the owner still in occupation. It turned out he was an eminent retired French neurosurgeon with excellent English conversational skills. I was thankful of this because my French is still classroom and John thinks he can speak French but it's just English with a French accent. He also laid out the most marvellous breakfast each morning, and we drank our coffee whilst watching the sunrise over Nice. Not a hangover in sight. Nice.

Shortly after we returned from Nice, I fulfilled a long-held dream and had my waist-length hair dreaded. With a nod to professionalism, I did not leave my hair to dread naturally, which would have been hella messy, but instead had a lovely lady come and create them with a crochet hook. This process took a whole day, was painful, and at the end of it my waist-length hair was just above my shoulders. That felt so good. So right. Not everyone was as enamoured with my baby dreads, but I did not give a hoot, and largely the patients, again, did not notice. As it turned out, they were hella messy for nearly three years as they went through their teenage phase before settling. The dread journey is a great ego leveller.

My dreads are mature and natural now, having brushed out most of the crochet work over the proceeding five years. I became quite a dread bore initially, it's a pretty magical process. The hair behaves in a very specific way. It's not dirty stuck together hair as you might or might not imagine. Your hair moves in cycles of expansion, contraction, lengthening, shortening and rotation all by itself, no interference needed, much like the breath of life.

I also remembered why I had taken my piercings out so long ago. They were sore, inconvenient, and the one in my mouth cracked my teeth. I removed them once more. I could not resist a septum piercing though, and that remains with my ear lobes stretched to just 1cm, not yet past the elastic limit of no return. I was beginning to settle into my own tattooed, alcohol-free skin. I felt fabulous. Fabulous and expansive.

Part 3

Chapter 14

Time was flying by. It was late 2018 and the penultimate semester of my women's health course. I began to search in earnest for jobs vacant in New Zealand. The Osteopaths New Zealand website is great for this. I noted that many jobs remained advertised until they expired. This was great as it meant that there was a good pool of jobs to pick from, but not so good as it probably meant that New Zealand made it a relatively uncomfortable, time-consuming process to relocate to their shores. Not like back in the day, Alf told me, when they just let us walk in.

In my mind, there should barely be any jobs advertised as surely everyone would leg it to New Zealand given half the chance. I remember during my first year as an osteopathic student, we had a little essay to complete at the start, "How I see myself as an osteopath," in which I made the statement that I would eventually achieve my position of an osteopath in New Zealand. We then repeated the essay at the end of the final year, by which time I declared that I was going to be not only an osteopath but also a doctor of natural health in New Zealand.

Funny how things change over five years, not just external

factors but how you as a person change with learning, it is another magical process. I was changed. I had grown exponentially. I was not the same person that started the course five years ago. One thing that remained steadfastly the same though, I *was* going to be an osteopath in New Zealand.

One advert kept catching my eye. It was for a clinic in Nelson in the South Island. They had been advertising for over six months and their advert was due to expire. I had always liked the look of Nelson as I perceived it to be hippy central. As it turns out, there are definitely a few here but not all of them by any means. My Kiwi buddy Claire, that I had met and worked with when I was landscaping and she was on her overseas adventure, she lived close to Nelson, so that sealed the deal. I set the clinic in my sights. Even though they were advertising for a New Zealand based osteopath only, I knew resistance would be futile. I sent them an email.

Nope, we only want a Kiwi osteopath. None of us can be bothered with the immigration process. Mmmmmm. Not deterred, I informed them that I was coming to New Zealand (Whaaaaat? Was I really going to do this?) and would pop in for a coffee if they would be happy to meet with me. They agreed. I'm sure they thought I would not show. On closer inspection of this idea, I considered it bad form to fly off to the other side of the world and leave the family at home, so it also doubled as a family holiday of a lifetime. My family thought me a little bonkers but were swayed by the thought of a holiday in New Zealand. Time to get another credit card.

I also considered that it may be a slight overreach of my trust in fate, and that if I was really going to travel to the other side of the world for a coffee with some people who had made it clear that they did not want to employ me from the UK, then it would be pertinent to at least set up some interviews with other clinics so I could get into the country that way and work myself to Nelson in due course. Yes, that's it. That's how fate might do it.

So that's what I did, and before you knew it, I had arranged interviews in Rotorua, Hawkes Bay, Wairarapa, and Wellington, all in the more populated North Island of New Zealand. The Easter holidays were approaching and proved an ideal time to take a break from my Women's Health course. In March 2019, we jetted off on a budget Chinese airline – £350 each return, unreal. I loved having noodles for each meal. I love airplane food full stop, strange but true. I'm so pleased and grateful that someone brings me food that I haven't prepared. I didn't mind the lack of leg room; John is taller so it may have bothered him more, plus he had the bonus of our small boy climbing all over him as we had not been seated together, and small boy wanted to be with his dad – the only downside of flying budget. On the plus side, I got to sit on my own and watch movies. Alas, small boy aged two and a half, reverted to explosive pre toilet training era, and in Shanghai Airport we had to rinse all his pants, of which there were many, and let them dry over the balustrades while waiting for our connecting flight.

Proceeding our arrival in Auckland was a crazy fast expedition from the near top of the North Island (Auckland Airport) to the bottom (Wellington Ferry). Logistically laid out according to distance and geographical location of my next interview. We picked up our hire car, a large, luxurious by our standard, people carrier, and made our way to our first overnight stop in Auckland: a nice suburban house Air BnB, nothing special but perfectly adequate. The part of Auckland we briefly experienced felt like just another big, busy city.

We made our first driving booboo by parking facing oncoming traffic. That's a no-no. To appease the children and because we were shattered, we found the nearest McDonalds before retiring to bed to the sound of the teenagers discussing the differences between UK and NZ MaccyDs. What a great introduction to cultural differences.

Up the next day, we were happy to be making our way out of Auckland and be on our way to Rotorua, 215km away, roughly a three-hour drive. Auckland is busy, but make no mistake, it is nothing like driving in the UK and certainly not the high pressure of driving around London. Coming from the UK, driving in New Zealand is quite serene and just heavenly once Auckland is behind you. The roads are open and clear, the sense of space is just incredible. The stifling compressive weight of humanity from the UK lifts from you; you can breathe once more.

Traveling southeast, you can smell Rotorua before you see it. An inland town approximately 65km from the northeast coast. It is a place of distinctive smell due to the abundance of hydrogen sulphide produced by the geothermal activity in the area. Although off-putting at first, I am told that you soon become nose blind to it and it's totally worth it for the natural bubbling mud pools, shooting geysers, and hot springs. It obviously does not put off the 77,000 people that live there. An absolute mecca for outdoor enthusiasts, we would soon learn that the whole of New Zealand is.

The clinic that I interviewed at was lovely and the people were lovely, but they expected a turnover of 50 patients per week from me, which was not really on my agenda. It had been a long time since I saw 10 patients per day, and I have never done it five days a week. That's an "only in an emergency" kind of number for me. If I was to churn through 50 patients a week, spending time in the upper and lower worlds whilst managing family life, I would become a shadowy husk of myself. All of this would be for the minimum amount of dollar required for the visa process. I needed to earn a salary of $55,000 to be eligible for my visa. The UK equivalent of £27,000 a year. As an enticement, I was told that any patients over that number would be a bonus for me. I can assure you that any patient over that number per week would not be a bonus for me or for the patient on the receiving end. This is purely down to the way I work and the life I lead. Each practitioner is very different. Not for me though. Strike one.

We spent the night after the Rotorua interview at Lake Taupo, about an hour drive from Rotorua and located in the centre of the North Island, enjoying the public thermal pools and our own private one in our accommodation. It all felt so very decadent and exhilarating. The pools themselves felt so strange and new. Palm trees, strange birds, steamy waters. Smiles all round amidst the fritz.

We set off the next morning for Napier in Hawkes Bay, New Zealand's art deco capital on the east coast, 155km away. Here I met with a thoroughly lovely chap who always seemed to have an advert running. Indicating either a high turnaround of staff or just a severe lack of osteopaths in New Zealand. After meeting with him I decided on the latter.

I did have a moment, not realising how different New Zealand's roads were and that we should adjust the Google travel estimates to allow more time, we found ourselves running late. I phoned to apologise and were urged to hurry as he was going out. My head very nearly exploded. Sorry bud, but we've just travelled from the other side of the world, have not had time to draw breath, and are making our way as quickly as possible through unfamiliar surroundings and on *very* twisty roads. When we finally arrived though, he was a *thoroughly* nice chap.

We got along very well in the interview, and he recommended a lovely local restaurant for lunch that provided beautiful, fresh food. Simple things done very well. Sitting there in the sunshine, we all just smiled, unable to quite comprehend that we were here in this beautiful place. Cicadas, sunshine and palm trees. We had landed in paradise.

We were also instructed not to leave until we had visited Te Mata Peak. Being able to drive up saved us time and afforded us fantastic views across the fertile Heretaunga plains of farms and vineyards stretching across the east coast to the Pacific Ocean. Big clear skies of the brightest blue only added to the sense of space and freedom. Te Mata Peak, a razorback mountain range, was a lovely introduction to the varied topography of New Zealand and a must do for the 360-degree view of the Hawkes Bay region. If you are lucky, you will spot Mount Ruapehu, an active volcano, some 200km away in the distance. We were too rushed to comprehend fully what we were seeing, having to move on too quickly. Definitely a place to revisit.

Before we left Hawkes Bay, a second interview was arranged for when we travelled back up at the end of our trip. I left feeling encouraged but with a nagging sense that I was too self-assured, too long in the tooth, too assertive for this position. I felt I would not take well-intentioned direction very well. That I might not be enough of a team player. Strike two.

That very same day, we continued to Carterton in the Wairarapa, some 240km further south, for my third interview. Beautiful, expansive farming country with an enveloping mountainous backdrop, 55km inland from the nearest beach on the east coast. Given that just up the road from where we come from in the UK, there is a sign indicating the furthest point from the ocean you can possibly be in the UK, I hoped that we would be coastal based in New Zealand.

Despite the land compromise, the lady was so lovely, and the job would be completely autonomous with fair pay. A happy strike three. We would think on it. Alas, this day was not yet finished! If I had been more aware of New Zealand's roads, I would have planned this differently, with infinitely more overnight stops. You *must* add more time to Google travel estimates.

Our next night was to be spent in Upper Hutt on the outskirts of Wellington. Another 53km southwest over Remutaka Hill, the northern end of the Remutaka Range which is the North Islands most southern mountain range. The hill itself is 725m high, and I thought it was pretty scary stuff driving over. I had never driven a mountain range before. The height, the twists, the drop offs only added to my fritz. It was breath takingly beautiful though, with tree covered peaks rolling off into the distance.

We arrived at our overnight stay in darkness. I have never been so pleased to flop into bed. I think the others concurred. Bear in mind that John does not drive, so by this time I was as frazzled as my dreaded hair.

The next morning we set off for my final interview of the North Island with the owner of a clinic in Wellington, a mere 35km southwest. A great interview in which we were invited into her house and walked upon the local hills with their family and dog. I was not too enamoured with the prospect of working in the capital city but could be swayed with the right enticement. As it happens, the decision was made for me. It would be required that I see a large amount of patients per week for less money than was required to obtain the visa. I'm sure she was aware of this. Maybe it was her polite way out. Strike four.

We finally made our way to the ferry for the cross over to the South Island for our "holiday" and what would be my final interview. Not an actual interview though, because they didn't intend to employ me, just a cup of tea, in Nelson. I'm sure they barely gave me a thought, but for me, so much rested on this meeting.

I was so pleased to sit on that ferry and not be driving. I think I drove just over 850km in a little over two days, had four interviews straight off the back of flying halfway across the world with my bedraggled family. Jet lag? No time for that. As luck and fate would have it, and because you see everyone you know all over New Zealand, all of the time, my best Kiwi buddy Claire was also on the ferry making her way back from a Wellington event. I'm not sure, but I think her first words to me were possibly, "F**k me, your hair's a mess."

Chapter 15

The very best antidote (other than seeing my buddy) to a billy bonkers journey across the world followed by an insane car journey through the North Island is … a bloody long walk. Three days after landing in the South Island and getting all our gear together, we embarked on a 60km stretch of the Abel Tasman National Park. A bookable New Zealand great walk, of which there are ten. This one is situated at the top of the South Island, starting from Marahau and winding its way along the coast through natural and regenerating forest to the stunning Wainui in the northern end of the park. Golden sandy beaches, turquoise ocean, stunning rock formations, and a marine reserve teeming with wildlife. What more could you wish for?

Claire was fabulous, helping us arrange our packs and food drops at each nightly location. A water taxi that ferried tourists into the park each day would also drop our packs with our clothes and sleeping bags and food provisions on the beach near our next stop each day. This meant we could walk with just day packs. Just blissful. We stayed in remote Department of Conservation (DOC) huts situated along the stunningly beautiful Tasman Coast; the walk tamed by the fact that if you were to have an incident, water taxis are at hand. We chose to end our route, as many do, at Totaranui where the water taxi service ceases, a mere 45km of unrelenting paradisical beauty. I think Claire still thought we were a little bonkers with a toddler in tow. It was a multiday hike as all the great walks are. Four days walking with three nights hut accommodation along the route.

We have since completed that great walk in its entirety. The northern end being the most beautiful if there even is such a thing. And boy, that walk was so freaking beautiful, astonishing. I had to keep pinching myself. The track itself was well kept as we came to expect from well managed great walks. Around every corner, looking out through towering tree ferns, you get glimpses of tropical looking islands rising out of the crystal-clear, turquoise waters. Abundant bird life, yellow crowned parakeets known as Kakariki are prevalent at the Bark Bay site, squawking joyfully overhead. The constant, ever present thrum of ciccadas if we ever needed reminding that we were in a foreign paradise. And a strange, cheeky ground dwelling bird, looked to be a throwback from the Jurassic period with its brown feathers, dark, beady eyes, and a sharp beak. We soon learnt these wekas are notorious for stealing anything you left within their vicinity that they could carry. You have been warned. In our time getting to know the weka, we have lost tea towels, ground coffee, tangerines, bowls, cutlery, toothbrushes, and most importantly, Walker's "Sooky", a blanket bear he has had since birth, luckily recovered from said birds' nest after a good (traumatising) game of hunt the bear.

Walker was a trooper through this tramp and walked a good portion. When he tired, he simply went in the child carrier on John's back. We were walking during the shoulder seasons summer/

autumn and the weather was mostly with us. We had the added bonus of less tourists (the irony of us also being tourists is not lost on me) on the track. Tourists pay a premium to walk the great walk tracks, the money raised going towards the upkeep of the tracks that can be hit by weather events and succumb to frequent land slips, and of course conservation. The introduction of foreign species, namely rats and possums, has caused havoc amongst the natives.

You can never be 100% sure of the weather in New Zealand so you must pack for every eventuality. We had one rainy morning and set off early from our hut at Bark Bay. Bark Bay remains one of my favourite stops on the Abel Tasman. Watching the stingrays through the waves at sunset on a pristine beach as the children splash in the shallows does it for me every time.

The other walkers in the hut, all adults, in awe of us walking with the children, were going to wait out the weather and get to the next hut later. We couldn't risk that though with Walker (aptly named) wanting to walk a lot, it took us time to cover the distances. This stretch is one the older children always reminisce over whenever the Abel Tasman is up for discussion. Walking the golden curve of Onetahuti Beach, the monsoon like rain lashing our faces, raincoats discarded as we laughed and twirled our way across the sand. Blessed be, how lucky were we.

I think what John will mostly remember from that day was having to double back after arriving at the last hut because I was sure our bag drop was further back up the track. I did feel sheepish when Claire, who was walking the last leg with us, stepped off a boat with our bags and freshly cooked food and John was a couple of kilometres back up the track, having waded across open water to find our non-existent bags. I think he was mollified by the fact that he found a fresh coffee at Awaroa Lodge, a beautiful retreat in the park for those that like a touch of luxury in paradise.

My favourite anecdote from that hut was a fabulous, young French hiker who was the first to the hut. He was attempting to light the fire and get his clothes dry. It transpired that he had walked this far with a heavy sack of carrots, a few apples, some tins of tomatoes he couldn't open, and a bottle of red wine he was willing to share in exchange for heartier fare. I assured him that he would be welcome to any of ours once it arrived, but fortune was in his favour. The arrival of a lovely young lady with peanut butter wraps was a far more enticing prospect, and his wine was duly shared elsewhere. Not that that bothered us (me), I had been sober for well over a year.

Our holiday finished with a glorious trip down the wild West Coast, staying at Gentle Annie campground in Mokihinui, based at the mouth of the mighty Mohikinui River. Crystal clear waters run from the native clad mountains to the wild thrashing waters of the Tasman Sea. We soon learnt that these incredibly beautiful, sacred places had their own form of protection from human invasion: sandflies. We were wholly unprepared for the sandflies. I do not recall anyone warning us either. They *loved* me and Edie and Walker. The intense itching waking you at midnight. I would literally be cross eyed with scratchiness. DEET remained the single most effective deterrent. I have tried so many natural remedies but some of us are just too tasty. I have since found some fabulous, home-grown, natural remedies. Or maybe with time, I have just made peace with the sandies.

The end of our trip culminated with a cup of tea at the osteopaths in Nelson. We were staying with Claire, about an hour from the small city of Nelson. It is classed as a city because it has a cathedral, it is really town sized. I was tired and flustered and managed to take out the wing mirror of the rental van as I reversed out of Claires drive. Doh! Right at the end of our trip, too. That would prove to be an expensive (£500) knock.

Our girls were trying out a local school for the day while I had my cup of tea. We dropped the girls at an intermediate school (aged 11–13) in Stoke, the next town along from Nelson. It was hard to get an idea of where they would attend if I pulled this off. The schools in Nelson were single sex colleges, and coming from the UK, I presumed they were private and we would not be able to afford that. Fortuitously, next door was a kindergarten, and we took advantage of this to drop in and have a look for Walker.

The gate had a latch to stop the children from escaping, but we were free to walk in. A lovely change to the prison style childcare facilities of home. We had not made an appointment but were welcomed in and shown around. What struck us was the amount of outdoor space and the children having freedom to roam in and out all day long. There were a group of, I would say 4-year-olds, concentrating in the corner.

"What are they doing?" we asked.

"They are cutting and using the glue gun. Don't worry, they only burn themselves once."

On closer inspection, you could see the children had access to all sorts of crafts: full blown scissors, wood, hammers, nails, and saws. Just to clarify, kindy is up to age 5 or 6. We loved it from the get-go. Common sense NZ: 1, health and safety UK: 0.

We headed into town to find a parking space. Comical to look back on now. Nelson is so easy to find a park. But we took the Great

British view of stressing to find a parking space … we duly found one. Walker and John headed off for a coffee, and I made my way to my interview (not interview).

It had been rearranged to coincide with their morning tea break. They were thoroughly pleasant folk. Nice tea. Nice cake. It was a large practice and not everyone made it to tea break, but all seemed accounted for. I regaled them with our dashing adventures across the North and South Island, but through all of the chatter, my hopes of securing work were dwindling. Pleasant conversation was not transmuting into a job offer. But I had felt so sure it would. Deep down I *knew* it would. Hmm. What was occurring?

And then the door opened and a friendly looking face appeared. They introduced Alf, freshly returned from a break in Australia. And you know what Alf said? He said he would go through the visa process and bloody employ me. *Holy mackerel.* I found out later that one of Alf's sons has dreads. I reckon they totally sealed the deal.

The rest of the trip was a stressy whirlwind (me) as we took the three-hour ferry journey in reverse and made a mad dash back up through the North Island to catch our plane home. Reportedly the most beautiful ferry journey in the world—with regular dolphin and whale sightings as you make your way through the Marlborough Sounds, a stunning area comprising a multitude of small remote native islands with golden sand beaches—I cannot remember much of the journey. I think by this point I was completely overloaded. The sheer beauty of New Zealand, the desire to be able to move there, not being totally in control of the outcome and having to rely on another to realise my dream was a test for my fortitude.

Fortunately, during the short time I spent having tea and cake with Alf, I surmised that he was a thoroughly nice chap.

Uber friendly, super chilled and laid back. That was a good sign considering my life, our lives, were now in his hands.

Poor Alf. He didn't realise what he had let himself in for.

≈ ★ ≈

Now, as I may have said before, I had been following Immigration New Zealand (INZ) for many years. I had seen the points required for entry go up and up. I had seen the rules change for work visas over the years. Right here, right now with Alf's offer of a job, I had enough points to apply straight for residency. I asked Alf if he would support my application, and he agreed to. Happy days. How long could it take? I had been correlating various documents and evidence as part of our Australia application. I knew it wasn't going to be a walk in the park, but on the other hand, I had not quite expected so much … resistance, so many hurdles.

I knew that the first step to getting a visa would be to get registered with the osteopathic governing body in New Zealand before I could even start the visa process. I had pre-empted this, was uber organised and had arranged a meeting to get the ball rolling. On the way back through Wellington, I called into the Osteopathic Council New Zealand (OCNZ) to hand deliver them my paperwork that I had been organised enough and had the foresight to take over with us. This paperwork would enable me to register as an osteopath in New Zealand. I cannot remember exactly the issue (illness I believe) but there was no Osteopathic Council member there to help me and a lovely lady from the Nursing Council was doing her best to facilitate my needs. I was missing my original police clearance. I had not thought to bring it as we must declare each year in the UK to renew our registration. I had it though, I had requested it as part of my Australia application. I phoned home and had Gary email it to OCNZ. Sorry, not acceptable. They would like to see the original. This meant that I could not immediately progress my registration and I would have to wait until we got home. Ahh! The pain of it all … this was only the start of the visa roller coaster.

    I had to wait patiently until we got home, whereby I obtained a verified copy of my police certificate and popped the original in the post to NZ. I could not progress my visa application without my registration. How long would snail mail take? To try to speed things up, I emailed OCNZ with my solicitor stamped verified copy and asked them to consider accepting that as my original wend its way across the world. I also had to pay the registration fee of $900 NZD. Even though I was stressing and impatient, things were happening. Alf had got my contract for work sorted and at the end of April 2019 the registrar approved my registration. Just over three weeks of tortuous waiting, which with hindsight was not actually too bad. Nevertheless, my nerves were already shot.

Chapter 16

On arriving back in the UK, I returned to my women's health course, and I graduated that June with an "Outstanding" accolade (I think we all did). I continued to work from my *huge* clinic in Tring. I was so fortunate to have a wide variety of patients to grace my door to keep me occupied during the visa application process.

I remember a young lad. He had been accused of a heinous crime and was so weighed down by his traumatic experience that his system was wound so tightly. When I put hands on, his system exploded with relief as it began to unwind. It would appear to the onlooker that I may have had superhuman strength because he lifted himself from the table and in some moments appeared to levitate before collapsing back down with a sigh, a release.

It was with this patient that I first saw a ball and chain attached to his ankle. Some people can drag this around with them after experiencing a trauma so strong that they disassociate with it. They are doomed to lug it around with them for all eternity. Unless they get the necessary help or can find it in themselves, when the time is right, to make a shift. A shift towards wholeness and a subsequent raise of vibration. Someone or something of the necessary vibration or wavelength can help you to integrate your pain, your experience, so that you make a shift towards health. A physical, emotional, mental, or spiritual shift. One does not work in isolation of another; you make a shift in one, they all shift.

I also had the pleasure of treating other healers, and one experience remains with me. It was when I became the proud owner of my second set of wings. Yes, a second set to accompany my huge upper angel ones. I was treating a lovely Irish lady who had a magnificent set of her own angel wings. I treated her often over a period and would always see other worldly figures as they looked on and lent their own healing gifts to the session.

During one session, I felt a tingle down my spine and at the level of the dorsal lumbar junction (DLJ). In line with the thoracic diaphragm, a pair of pink, sparkly fairy wings materialised, markedly smaller than the angel set. Well, if you thought having a single set of angel wings was incredible, I was blown away to receive a second set of different energetic origin. Spirit, the gift that keeps on giving.

I have not done too much research into my wings. I find it can cloud what you know to be inherent truth. I just accept them as is. Trust your knowing, your intuition, and wisdom. I have seen enough to know there is always more to learn and am grateful for the opportunity to be doing so. To be well and truly and firmly on my own path of healing.

I see them as a process of levelling up. When you have reached a certain frequency, cleared enough of your karmic dogma you are able to access energetic realms of differing origin. I see the largest set at the top of the spine as the primary energetic source and the lower ones (yes, pleural) as contributing but to lesser extents as they make their way down your spine. This is my present innate knowing of the subject matter.

Anyway, I digress. I have treated this whole family, including the dog. The little dog was brought in because it had never eaten well, struggled to open his bowel, and was absolutely terrified of the vets. I advised to stop all medications, untwisted the little chap's gut and bowel, and he was the very best he had ever been. He reclaimed a puppy like, joyful demeanour with a grand appetite and the most excellent bowel movements.

One of their young daughters had the gift, and I left her with my healing books that had been so enlightening for myself when my own healing journey started; RIP Barbara Brennan, an extraordinary healer. When we left for New Zealand, they gifted me a beautiful silver necklace of angel wings, and I still have the certificate of excellence the young girl made for me taking pride of place in my clinic.

It was often the way: you treated the mother, then the children, then the father, then the grandparents, and then the pets. I've got to say, chasing cats around my oversized treatment room was a hoot and far more challenging than my toddler sessions. I swiftly learnt that cats preferred to be treated in their own homes. As with any being, once you connect with a cat at a deeper level, they will happily give themselves over to the treatment session. You just have to catch them first.

Easier to catch are babies. Many babies. The birthing process, although natural, can come with its own pressures and strains which at times leave an imprint upon the baby. Especially in situations of trauma or medical intervention. For example, simple treatments that release restrictions imposed by forceps will lead to improved suckling, rest, and digestion. Such satisfying and gratifying experiences for not only mother and baby but for myself. Simple pleasures.

These kinds of experiences and amazing people kept me going through the bonkers, stressful journey of the New Zealand visa application. Immigration NZ are a force to behold and completely a law unto themselves. If you ever intend to do these visas for yourself, make sure you get up on NZ employment law. I thought we had. There is a very good website which seemingly makes everything very clear but must change with relative frequency. Over the course of the year, poor patient Alf had to revise the work contract numerous times. It got very confusing on my computer with files declaring "work contract final", "work contract final, final", "work contract definite final" and so on. This literally went on until a couple of weeks before our visas were granted.

Weeks would pass and you would think you had it in the bag and that this contract was definitely bona fide 100% legally correct. And then the mail of doom would drop into your box with something along the lines of: "You do not get paid for a 15-minute smoko (NZ tea break, not necessarily for smoking) so cannot claim that as working time; therefore, you are under the requisite hours for a full time employee," and so on and so on. These mails would also include the dreaded line, "If we do not receive … within 1–2 weeks, your application will be terminated," or something to that effect. These emails would always send me into a dizzying, whirling dervish of monumental stress. I dreaded them. It did not help that your case officer can and often does change at the drop of a hat, and each new case officer has their own set of interpretations of NZ law and immigration expectations. Ridiculously exasperating.

I was eternally grateful that I worked in a profession (health) which could be fast tracked, and I use that term *very* loosely. If you have ever emigrated in recent years, I'm sure you are well versed in the support groups available online. For myself they were mostly on social media. You get to know others that are applying at the same time as yourselves and you can share and support in the glory and misery of the journey you are all on. If you were not in a fast-tracked profession at the time of applying, I think the waiting time to receive a case officer was 18 months plus, it may even have been two years. Tortuous. I'm not sure I would have coped with the wait. I was eternally grateful that we had a case officer at all, even if the rules appeared to change on a weekly basis.

You would think that someone with the gift of seeing and knowing that what she desired would eventuate would be able to rest easy in the knowledge that everything would be okay and would not get so wound up with stress. I'm not sure what it is, but even though I know deep down in my soul that all will be well or is at least as it should be, I cannot refrain from losing my shit in times of stress. Absolutely no decent coping mechanisms at all. Maybe I used alcohol as a coping mechanism for so long that I still needed time to adjust, rebalance, and learn new ones.

Wings or no wings, I was still a mortal stress monkey.

Chapter 17

Understandably, prior to moving to New Zealand, you must prove a lot of other stuff to INZ.

I had to prove who I was to begin with. Simple enough, right? Not if you have gone by four different surnames. Time was spent finding not only my own divorce certificates but also the ones of my parents ... this was just the beginning.

I had to prove my de facto relationship was real. We both had to write a chronology of our relationship. Thank God for social media, you won't hear me say that often. It provided a visual representation of our relationship from the very beginning, our trips away, and all the beautiful procrastination tools that we shared. Sorting our life out through the media of inane quizzes on Facebook with titles such as "What colour soul is your dog?" (maybe I would have achieved a first for my degree if I had done more research and less procrastination of this nature).

All our social media online interactions were saved. Reams of conversation printed for delectation and delight of our case officer. I have a habit of not deleting anything. Some of my friends cannot bear it when they see 2,438 emails on my phone, but it certainly comes in handy … you never know when you might have to refer to that particular email. My iPhone SE, which I bought second-hand and cannot bear to replace, has every single photo I've ever taken since the birth of Walker in 2016. I was able to go through and screenshot pictures that the phone had already timed and dated for me and make a material timeline family album of our relationship. After it had been posted, received, and certified by INZ, it made a lovely gift for John's mum.

We needed copies of any shared bills and responsibilities. Not too hard you would think, but I hadn't bothered to put John on the electric or gas bills, etc, so that took time to arrange with the relevant companies. Luckily, we had working tax credits together after Walker was born. So many finickity little things that you do not think of and are not made aware of. The support groups are great for ideas of ingenious ways to prove INZ requests.

Friends in the UK and New Zealand wrote in on our behalf confirming our relationship, how they knew both of us and for how long. These testimonies had to be witnessed and signed by a Justice of the Peace (JP). Some of our wonderful friends did this twice, once for Australia and once for New Zealand. Relationship confirmed.

I had to prove that I was of good character. No drama. I've never been in trouble (properly) with the law, and I had to get my police certificate to get registered as an osteopath. Nothing to worry about. However, INZ required some super-duper in-depth police certificate, the one used for my registration was not sufficient. No worries. How do I go about that. Ah yes, I see. It takes how long? Bloody hell. So, I sent off for that and waited for my shinier than shiny police certificate to come back. Our application could not proceed until that was in.

After two months I received my police certificate, but it was not shinier than shiny. It has on it a DUI from the morning after my 21st birthday. Easily done you might think if you are young and stupid (or alcoholic in my case). Sufficient time had passed for it to be removed from my normal police certificate. I had long forgotten about it. Surely they could not judge me for an action carried out over twenty years ago. Wrong. Judged. Now I had to really prove that I am of good character. It was not enough apparently that I had obviously sorted my shit out and was now an upstanding professional member of society.

Cue further affidavits from friends and members of our local community, namely the village Vicar (previously the village publican) who had known me from year dot, plus those of professional colleagues. I had also saved a certificate I had received after completing a drink awareness course which shortened my driving ban considerably. It was in a shoe box along with my Mensa certificate and my Chelsea Flower Show medal, the important stuff. It was all good, I was clearly contrite, wished to change my ways and had paid my dues at the time. God forbid I am ever recovered enough to write the prequel. Good character confirmed.

We weren't finished though. We now had to prove we were in good health. Simple you would think. No. There are only a few INZ approved clinics in the country. They are miles away. Very fully booked with huge wait lists. Everyone over the age of 12 also had to have an x-ray. We got our slot and trotted off for our physical exam, eye exam, and x-ray. We all passed and awaited our clearance certificates from the clinic. Everything takes time, a killer for one so impatient. And wouldn't you know it, whilst we were waiting for our visas, Edie turned 12. So we had to go back up and do it all again. Joy. Eventually, health confirmed.

⋛ ★ ⋚

We (I) desperately needed respite from the relentless visa application. So during the summer of 2019 we drove to the Ardeche in France for a family camping trip. Camping is a relatively cheap holiday, and in the south of France you have guaranteed sunshine, unlike the UK, and it is much more cost effective to amuse yourself in the sunshine. The channel tunnel under the ocean makes a quick connection from the UK to France, and there were always discount fares to be found. A good adventure to be had.

I was so stressed out though. I remember having the biggest cold sore erupt on my lip, so big that it was painful to talk or eat. Everything done with a straw. Lovely. Not to worry, respite was at hand. We were going to relax in the sunshine wilderness of mountainous France, and I couldn't wait.

We arrived in France, set up camp and had a jolly good first week or so. We swam in the wild clear river below the camp, running the small rapids in our inflatable; spent time meandering around the local markets practising our very pidgin French to the amusement of the stall holders. Time slowed down in France as we breathed the beautifully fresh air and tried to forget about the visa for a short period of time.

Alas, escaping to the south of France did not mean escaping the visa process. I should not have opened the email. Towards the end of the second week, I received an email from INZ requesting a court order to prove I was allowed to take my (our) children to New Zealand to live.

Surely this was all sorted ages ago. Gary and I got on very well and were in complete agreement. We had been to the solicitors, had it all written up, signed, and witnessed. Nothing more to see here. This had been a familiar process for others in my support group that had divorced and wished to emigrate. We knew what needed to be done. I had read the INZ manual pertaining to this very important aspect of our move and had done everything by the book. It turns out that our case officer interpreted the rules differently. This was an absolute kicker. Surely all case officers would interpret the rules the same. Not so. And guess what, we had two weeks to get our court order in or they would cancel (or words to that effect) our application. I wish I had known the Serenity Prayer then. I thought my head might explode. I drove like a madwoman to get back to England. It wasn't until we reached the top of France that the children noticed a large cricket living in my hair. That's how crazy I was. A crazy cricket lady.

We got back to England, and I immediately contacted a solicitor. The consensus was that as Gary and I were friendly and in complete agreement, a court order was not necessary and would not be granted. We would not even get a hearing. Upon begging and pleading and showing them the INZ correspondence, one agreed to take us on with a £5,000 deposit and a further £5,000 on completion. It would take upwards of eight months to get a hearing. F**k. We didn't have anywhere near that amount of money, and we didn't have eight months. We had two weeks. Shit.

I cancelled all work, and I sat in my clinic day after day, night after night reading family law. During my youth I had completed one year of a law degree. I felt totally out of my depth but just knew I could do it. Once I become obsessive, shit gets done. I am a perfectionist control freak. I would tick all those boxes dagnabbit. I had to fill in a C100 Child Arrangements Application and I wrote up our own Child Arrangement Consent Order and relevant declarations using all the correct legal jargon.

I rang up Watford Court and I begged. We received a C21 Urgent Directions Order:

"Upon reading the C100 application of Kelly Ann MacNeill, dated 29 July 2019, and in view of the unusual circumstances and urgency, the court is willing to consider the application but requires the attendance of both parties at court, but in the absence of either party, it being understood that the respondent, Gary MacNeill, is supporting the application.

The Court Orders:

1. The application will be listed on short notice and be heard by a Circuit Judge at 2pm on 2 August 2019 at Watford Family Court, Cassiobury House, Watford (TE 30 minutes). Both parties shall attend court at 1.30pm
2. The applicant, Kelly MacNeill, shall urgently serve the application and this order on the respondent, Gary MacNeill."

We had everything documented: how often the children and Gary would see each other, how often they would talk to each other, how the girls would keep in contact with his family, how we would deal with financial issues, how we would make important decisions, religious considerations, where we would live, where the girls would go to school, and so on. It was a massive document. All the new consent orders and statuary declarations were written in greater depth covering every eventuality and were witnessed and signed once more at our local solicitors.

Gary and I had our day in court. We looked out of place waiting to go in. No one to represent us and clearly getting along very well. There was a slight hiccup as we went through security to take our turn. I had forgotten a pair of knickers in my handbag. It had been a hot summer, and those pants were not cotton. It made the security chuckle as he pulled out my frillies.

In court I was so nervous and sat and stood at all the wrong times. The judge reiterated how very unusual this situation was, but he would basically humour us. I was honoured that he decreed my paperwork top class, and, on that basis, he would grant us our court order. Hammer down. Sorted.

Or so we thought.

The court order came through relatively quickly, and I had it emailed directly to INZ with a further certified copy winging its way in the post. Could you believe that. A massive pat on my back, thank you, Lord. Massive gratitude to Watford Court and the presiding judge. We got that court order in right on the two-week mark and for the princely sum of £350. Stoked.

It was not to last though. INZ got back to us and declared: it did not have the judges signature on it. They would not accept it. You have got to be shitting me. It has the bloody royal stamp of the crown court. Nope, not good enough. But that's what a court order looks like here from the UK. Nope, not good enough.

At this point, my wider family were telling me I should just give up. New Zealand clearly doesn't want you. They knew me well though … quitting was not an option. They were completely bemused by it all. I had taken to walking everywhere with a massive stack of papers under my arm, just in case.

With extreme embarrassment, I contacted the judge's private secretary. This was wholly unprecedented and unheard of, and she wasn't sure how the judge would respond to that request. The document was just and legal and we were lucky to have had so much of his time already. Shiiiiiit. I could not pester him. She could only present it to him and see what he would do.

I held my breath for what felt like an age. Six weeks later it came back signed. As there was no designated place for a signature, the judge had eloquently and lavishly signed his name across the bottom of the document. A certified copy made again and into the post. Email sent. Right to remove children confirmed.

This was by no means everything. Just the big ones that stick in my mind. The amount of paperwork and toing and froing. Writing/begging this person and that. A lot of goodwill was shown to me, people that went out of their way to help when they had no reason to, in England and New Zealand. A huge debt of gratitude is owed to them. Especially a local lawyer who I imposed myself upon through his friendship and connection with my maternal family. The amount of documents I had to copy and verify was staggering. It was a costly, time-consuming mission. The last bundle I took in was as thick as my arm. Hundreds of documents. Each one normally costing £5. He would do them for a donation to his office kitty. It took him hours. I was so grateful, but on my way out he graciously asked that I never return to his office.

INZ was not yet finished with me; my personal favourite was yet to come. Another heart stopping email arrived in my account: we need more proof that you are an osteopath that does osteopathic work. Heart stopped. Head exploded. I was just mush and vapour. I was frightened that I may lose myself in this process. I was not sure that my emotional and mental fortitude would prevail.

Whilst I had gathered myself, the metaphorical act of pulling up my socks and putting my big girl pants on, I tried to think logically. I had already sent them (all certified copies of course) and made them aware of:

- My qualifications – i.e my degree certificate and transcript
- My General Osteopathic Council (UK) registration
- My new Osteopathic Council New Zealand registration
- My new job offer and contract in New Zealand
- My yearly accounts since qualification and registration – tax returns from Inland Revenue
- Record of various continued professional development (CPD) over the years including my recent two year post graduate diploma in Women's Health Osteopathy
- Affidavits from colleagues, clinic owners, receptionists
- My yearly subscription to the Institute of Osteopathy, our UK professional body
- My website and social media marketing
- My online booking system
- Every single monthly statement (bloody hard to find) from my Payment Sense card machine which I used to take payment from time of qualification and registration.
- Pictures of my clinic
- Past and present contracts for clinic space hire
- Evidence of my paying for room rent monthly

I was spent. I had run out of ideas. What else could I send them? I had to think outside the box. The idea came to me in a flash. Who best knows the osteopathic work I do? Why my patients of course. I contacted 50 of them and gave them the email address of my case officer and asked of them, if they had the time and inclination, if they would write in my defence. If they could outline why they see me (only if they wish) and how I have helped them (or not) osteopathically as an osteopath. And if they could, could they please make it within the next two weeks … I sat back exhausted. It was out of my hands now. I really did feel as if I was on trial.

I do not know exactly who wrote. Many told me they did and shared copies of their emails with me. I cried a lot. I felt truly humbled and blessed. One couple stood out. I had been treating the lady for a long time and she wrote me a beautiful testimonial. I had treated her husband a few times as well and knew he worked in the police force. It turns out he was a chief inspector with the London Metropolitan Police. After they received his testimony, sent from his work email account, an email dropped into my box to request that my patients stop writing to the case officer. Professional standing confirmed.

Chapter 18

Through every step of this process I did not turn back to drink, but I still managed to lose my shit on a regular basis. This was truly a baptism of fire for a newly sober person, having to learn new coping mechanisms under such duress.

Levelling up spiritually often denotes a change in habits and routines. We were not shopping in supermarkets anymore; the fake bright lights, crowds, incessant chatter and overall energetic thrum left me depleted and anxious. I could not stand the thought of going in one again. Fortunately, I had a light bulb moment when I realised I didn't have to go in. Just like that. Years of habit, gone. I started to shop at the local farm shop. Buying local and only what we needed.

I sold our TV. We rarely paid attention to the news, such depressing outpourings. The monotony of scrolling the guides each night and the inane loud chatter of youth programs grated on my soul. I was glad to see the back of it.

I became consistent with my yoga, I paid attention to my body for the first time in ages. All the good stuff. Stuff that I just would not think of when drinking. When I had to consider what I might do to relax without drinking, the thought of reading a book which

I used to love or having a bubble bath with candles was just too ridiculous to conceive of.

When I'm good, I'm *really* good, extremes of reality, no middle ground. I was not yet walking the neutral middle line, but I was well on my way to finding it within myself. The process of levelling up spiritually means that you are driven to improve yourself in ways that might not have previously appealed to you.

Nights of sobriety were filled with jigsaws, each getting more elaborate as the time went on. Great family time. Great for being present but I'm not sure the puzzling was a sufficient mechanism to combat the stress INZ inflicted upon me (which I inadvertently inflicted upon myself) and subsequently everyone around me.

When I was drinking, I could not think of anything more dire or boring than doing a puzzle. I did not factor in the joy of being present and connected with my family. Alcohol had only sought to separate me from my true self and those around me. Looking back, I am always gobsmacked at the ludicrous nature of addiction and what we tell ourselves. It is a severe affliction of the soul. Never mind the fact that I couldn't stop drinking, I honestly thought I might die of boredom if I did. I could not have been further from the truth if I tried. I was deeply grateful to have stopped with time to do the deeper work still required of self for further expansion of one's spirit.

It wasn't just the emotional stuff that I afflicted everyone with, it was also physical. It makes perfect sense that spirit might favour a clear vessel to work through. With my newfound sobriety and energetic level up, I felt a strong desire to cleanse my physical body from the inside out.

I took it upon myself to detox my armpits. I had no choice. When you poison yourself regularly you stink. There is no getting away from this fact. And to cover up that fact, you might use super strength anti-perspirant, which is not good for you and just retains all the toxicity that your system is trying to eliminate. Armpits sweat for a reason, but I had used antiperspirant for years in a bid to camouflage the toxic stench of alcoholism. Now it seemed that all the nasty stuff that I needed to expel, wanted to come out all at once. I was behaving healthily (ish), but once again I stunk. Really stunk. The action of levelling up energetically was causing me to purge my system.

Dropping alcohol often requires a period of replacing the lost sugar gained through drinking with other forms of sugar, and so a sweet tooth developed for a while. I did not beat myself up here. I knew my body would level out as it got used to life without alcohol. I had rode the initial pink cloud of sobriety I had read so much about, so prevalent in the early days. The pink cloud is where you cannot believe how good life is sober whilst also filling your face with Häagen Dazs ice cream. This was totally okay, and I indulged those particular cravings knowing that in time this new craving would pass, and it did. You do eventually come down off the pink cloud and have to learn to live in your real, unfiltered version of the world, sober. It takes some effort; I was getting there.

To detox more effectively I knew I had to persevere with no antiperspirant and my system would come right, but it was the high heat of summer, and I feared I would lose all my patients otherwise. I regularly implored "Excuse my stench, I'm detoxing." It was so hot; it became hard for me to be around my own armpits. After six weeks without antiperspirant, I did relent and used diluted essential oils as deodorant (far less harmful than antiperspirant IMO) and then as the cold weather began to set in, I once again began my detox in earnest. It took another eight weeks. I highly recommend doing it. I am still a bit stinky if I poison myself, especially with excess sugar, or if my hormones fluctuate wildly. Otherwise, I think I smell okay. You soon come to prefer the natural smell of bodies. Armpits are great indicators of general health and should *not* be silenced.

⇒ ★ ⇐

With the onset of winter, it was approaching the end of the year and we were keen to get the visa process wrapped up. We wanted to be in New Zealand before Christmas. I contacted INZ and they put it to me that it was likely our visas would be through by Christmas, but they couldn't guarantee it. Fair enough. They offered me to apply for the work visa. Although I had not initially wanted to go this route, they implied that I was likely to get it and our residency visas would follow shortly.

My grandmother had passed away and left all her grandchildren £1,000. This was the fee for the work visa. Universe/Grandma provides. I filled in all the forms and sent them all the required documents, it was not enough that they already had them in our residency application and awaited the verdict. It was October 2019. The turnaround was surprisingly swift for a change. Denied. The job advert did not *exactly* match my job contract. But they knew this, they already had the job advert. Could I please have my £1,000 back. No.

Meanwhile, Gary had booked plane tickets for January 2020. The plan was for us to arrive in the South Island and for him to follow and come and see our new home and help us settle in. I tried to temper his excitement; INZ were not to be relied upon, they did not work to anyone else's schedule. Christmas was fast approaching, and we had contact with our case officer right up to Christmas Eve. Christmas passed; I contacted INZ once again. Our case officer had promised us it would be completed prior to Christmas, I explained. They explained that our case officer had gone on holiday for *six weeks*. I had a meltdown. Alf had a meltdown. Management was contacted, and I give the nice lady her due, she really got things moving after a relatively short time. One issue: the contract needed re writing. You're kidding? Nope ...

Work contract final. Final. Final. Absolute *final* version 108 (slight exaggeration). Sent. Accepted. *Holy moly*.

I am astounded that I remained sober throughout this time. Hallelujah. Sobriety rocks.

Chapter 19

It was 4am, the sun yet to rise. John was working up north when I woke early as usual to check my email. My phone and laptop right beside me as I slept. This was a well-entrenched habit. Heart pounding, breath held. Elation or defeat? To receive nothing was the worst. Even worse than receiving a perceived negative email. If you received nothing you knew that whilst you were up and going about your day, the good people of New Zealand would be asleep. They would not be working in the INZ offices so you knew your chances of getting further mail was slim to none for the next twelve-hour period which would drag by, whereby I would then be in bed, struggling to sleep with immigration anxiety but desperately wanting to so I could wake up to check my mail once more. So it went on, the monotony and desperation of waiting for mail.

That morning though, there was mail. Dare I open it? Sweating and nervous, I clicked the button.

No need to worry today. Today was our (my) day. Tears of relief. With the utmost love and gratitude to INZ, our visas were finally approved 21st January 2020.

I could not believe that after nearly a year I had finally received the email that all would be emigrants are so desperate to receive. I had known it would eventually come but there was always the underlying anxiety that they would decline our application or that Alf, as patient as he was, would find someone else to fill my coveted role.

I sat on my own with this news. With John working up north and Gary rather ridiculously enjoying the North Island of New Zealand without us, the house was quiet. I lay in bed and just relished the news by myself. Hugging myself, crying my tears of relief.

It was 5am, the children were still asleep, but I could contain myself no longer. I crept into their room to wake them with the news. Edie cried. Not tears of happiness. The realisation that they would be parted from their dad, albeit for a short period of time, hit home. I am sure they never thought this day would come. I soothed them with the knowledge that their dad would be joining us shortly after we landed. We would not be parted for long.

I phoned John next, I don't think he could quite believe it either. Although he had lived through the trials and tribulations of the visa process, it was ultimately *my* fight for *my* dream, although he was happy to come if it eventuated. He would have to hand in his notice, a shock I'm sure to his company for whom he had worked for two decades. Not known for his impulsive deviations from the norm, they were quite surprised that it was actually happening.

Whilst Gary was away in New Zealand, we began to coordinate packing our lives up in the UK. He would arrive back in the UK before we left. We did not intend to take a lot with us. One backpack or suitcase each and an extra suitcase of paperwork and things of important sentimental value. Other more non-essential bits, but were still of importance, were stashed away with parents. At this point, as I sorted through all our paperwork and pictures, I regretted requesting that my dad burn so many photos a decade earlier. Photos of my earlier years. Evidence of teenage and 20s wasteland. All burned in a bid to heal in some way. Oh well, it was done now.

We aimed to leave in six weeks. Six weeks to pack up our lives, reduce them to such an extent that they could fit on our backs. It was a liberating thought; it was a mammoth feat.

We had very little money and the sale of our "stuff" would be funding the trip and helping us to set up in New Zealand. Friends, family, and members of our wider community knew we were trying to emigrate and had already put dibs on certain items of ours. Those items that we knew others particularly wanted we gave them or let them have for a very low price.

Next, we opened our home and garage and had people come in waves to choose at their leisure. A controlled home and garage sale. There were people that wanted our camping and hiking gear, this was hard and emotional to let go of, but we were sure that bio security would not allow it into New Zealand. Some wanted John's tools which were also hard for him to part with, but he did so with grace. Boy, does he wish he had brought them with us now. Even if we had wanted to ship them over though, we just did not have the money.

There are still some things now, small things that crop up every now and then, that I really wish we had brought with us. Silly little things like a particular cookbook with its stuck together pages and well fingered recipes that evoke strong emotions to this day. A pair of knee-high purple leather boots bought from Camden in my London living days that I cherished for so long, they would have been passed down to Edie or Lily – despite their protestations. Plus some Christmas decorations that had been with me since I had begun to put up my own tree.

Our rented council home was put on the market when we left the UK and it was surreal and saddening to see my Christmas Santa laying on the living floor with one broken, bent leg in the promotional pictures. Abandoned in our haste to pull it all together and leave on time.

What I really wished we could have brought with us though, was our animals, particularly my dog. I did not cry once before or after the move for anything or anyone other than my dog. Phoebe was a beautiful German Shepherd. I had her from a puppy. She was getting on, and the requisite medical procedures and the travel would have been hard on her. It would have cost more to bring her over than it cost to transport the entire family. Added to that, we were not allowed dogs at the accommodation we had lined up for our initial year, and all we heard from experienced tenants and estate agents was that dogs, especially big hairy ones, were not an enticing prospect for potential landlords and we would find it hard to secure a rental should we need to.

I left Phoebe with a great friend of ours. I cried and cried and cried. I can still feel the emotional, deep impact upon my heart when I take myself there, which I do all too frequently. Always afraid to ask how she is doing. Guilt for leaving her ever present.

Our cat, Tinkerbelle Scat Cat Coo MacNeill, was rehomed with my sister's mother-in-law and at the time of writing, is still living her best life in the lap of luxury.

Our other dog Ebsi, who had seen me through two marriages and two divorces, was put to sleep shortly before we came. He was nearly 20 years old. His back end was going, and he frequently lost control of his bowel and bladder. I was hoping that he would pass in his own time. Osteopathy and homeopathy kept him well into his latter years, and he was affectionately known as "the dog that wouldn't die".

Our chooks, including Betsy Blue, my fave, all found a lovely home with friends in a nearby village. From then on, I vowed, when we settled in New Zealand, to remain pet free for practically the first time in my life.

Saying goodbye to friends and family was a quiet affair. There were no great emotional drawn-out goodbyes. It happened slowly over the week leading up to our departure. It had been so long in the offing, I think they were kind of prepared, even if they didn't think it would happen. No worries though, we were off on a big adventure, and we would come back for visits. Best of all, they could visit us and have their own Kiwi adventure.

How little we knew and realised the complexity of this scenario.

Part 4

Chapter 20

We bid a final emotional farewell to Gary from our driveway one early, grey morning in late February 2020. He had kept his holiday in the North Island relatively short and would join us for an extended period in the coming April to see us settle in. It was our plan that Gary would spend six months over the summer period of each year in each country. Returning to the UK each time to earn money before returning once more to enjoy life with us.

We were flying out of London Heathrow over the February leap year dates, due to arrive in Nelson on the 3rd of March 2020. We had initially looked to book our flights through the east, but a virus, which we had not paid any attention to due to being knee deep in shifting continents, hampered those plans, and we flew though LA and Hawaii instead.

Lily was LA mad at the time, so we took the opportunity to stop over. The huge lanes of traffic on the six lane (each side) freeway and smog over the ocean really made a startling impact. If we thought the UK was busy, we were not prepared for this. The smog hung over the bright blue ocean like a grotty, grey rag, in complete juxtaposition to the friendly, chatty seals, and joyful, leaping dolphins we saw from the beach and pier.

We gave the children free rein, and they all found their churro limit quite quickly after being adamant that they could just keep eating them. You really can't. John and I tried a deep-fried onion; its layers petalled like a flower, reminiscent of my time working in hospitality. The actuality of it was not as I remember. Quite sickly in fact, plus all portions were supersized, overwhelmingly so.

We enjoyed people watching at the famous Venice Beach where we lazed on the golden sands and strolled through the popular market there. The skateboarders and roller bladers whizzing past on the Venice boardwalk; colourful folk, street entertainers and muscled fit folk bending and flexing in the sunshine. It was very enjoyable but so alien as a way of life to us. I'm quite sure Lily could have stayed there though. She loved everything about it.

Our layover was brief, just a couple of days, and we were happy to be on our way, having had a good dose of LA. The next leg of our trip on Hawaiian Air was most enjoyable. The flight attendants were bright and cheerful with their colourful uniforms and garlands of flowers around their necks, and so warm and welcoming. Great hospitality from the small island nation.

On arrival in New Zealand, we had a one-night stay in the Novotel at Auckland airport, the children in awe of their surroundings and the room service. We were up bright and early the next day, our body clocks all over the place. We crashed into Auckland's domestic terminal all stress and huffing (me), dragging our luggage behind us to catch our flight to Nelson. Fully prepared for queues and cancellations and deep frustrations (me again), we were happily disappointed. We made an impact as we made our way through the terminal to the waiting area. It was actually very straight forward. Just one waiting area for all flights.

As easy as it was, I was still a fritz ball of sympathetic stress, full on fight or flight mode, and it did not go unnoticed by the other waiting passengers. In fact, they positively gawked at us. Maybe it was my wild birds nest hair, maybe it was my shouty sweary. Maybe they could just feel the emanation, the culmination of a full year's stress monkey radiating from this crazy lady. I had not yet truly landed in New Zealand. My midline was definitely not in neutral. It was an oscillating wave way out to the left. I needed to chill. Out. Man.

We were only moving with a backpack each and an extra suitcase of important documents ... and a computer and printer. I should not have packed the printer; it did not work in New Zealand, but I had not known this and it was new and decent. I still have it in our garage, and now I must wait for a visitor with enough luggage allowance to send it back with. Oh, and don't waste space in your backpack bringing sentimental cushions. Actually, do if you want to, but just bring the cushion covers and refill them here. Unless you are shipping all of your stuff in a giant container, then ship everything you own and more. Including the kitchen sink.

My gorgeous buddy Claire had arranged for us to be picked up from Nelson Airport by one of her work friends who happened to be in the area. If I had realised how truly, ridiculously easy it was to get to anywhere in Nelson from the airport I would not have troubled her for a lift. Although it was nice to be met by a friendly face, a friend of my friend, and make a new connection. It would soon become apparent that everyone in Nelson, and quite possibly all New Zealand, are socially connected. Six degrees of separation in action right there.

We made our way to the house which was to be our home for our first year in New Zealand. We were renting the place from a lovely osteopath. She had been a godsend during the visa application time helping Alf and me and had retired from the practice I was starting at and was going overseas for a year.

It was a beautiful light weather board house in a smart leafy area. There was a playground and brook at the bottom of the driveway; the gardens had fruit trees, a thriving vegetable patch, and beautiful flowered borders. It was a quiet area close to the local catholic school which our girls would not be attending. I had investigated it while going through the visa process, but it was too hard to pass ourselves off as Catholics, even if it was a great school. Fortunately, we were spoiled for choice. All the schools in Nelson are pretty awesome and none too far away. It is a compact, small city.

It was a lovely home with everything one could need, and despite what we had heard regarding New Zealand homes, it was bright, dry and warm with not a spot of mould to be seen. It also had a TV, but we ignored it. We hadn't had a TV for two years now. Walker remained blissfully unaware. As for the girls, aged 11 and 12, they had gotten their first mobile phones, against my better judgement, so that they could stay in contact with their dad easily and effectively.

Claire and her lovely partner, Mark, came to greet us. We had not drunk alcohol in a long time, nearly two years, but overcome with all manner of emotions and jet lag, I had a Baileys … and possibly a champagne. How easily they slipped in, almost without thought.

All under control though. Just this one time. It was a celebration after all.

A meet and greet with the neighbours had been arranged on the green by the house courtesy of our lovely host osteopath, and we felt truly welcomed to the neighbourhood. A lovely spot to spend our first year.

≋ ★ ≋

Not one to give myself or the rest of the family a break or chance to settle into our new space, our first week was spent zooming around Nelson and surrounding area buying school uniforms and sorting out a kindy for Walker. Finances dictated to us, and we did not have the resources for a leisurely break.

While investigating the schools for the girls, I had also investigated kindergartens for Walker. It had been so hard to gain perspective from the UK. Some kindys had seemed much too far from my new workplace and our new home. Claire had visited a few for us that I deemed appropriate from the UK but did not vibe with us once we were here. We ended up going with one further out that I had discounted as being too far but was in fact only five minutes up the road. I would advise anyone emigrating to New Zealand to just chill. It's easy to arrange everything once you are here. There is enough to worry about home side. Don't make extra stress for yourself.

Looking back now, I'm not sure why I was so rushed to get him settled in kindy. Maybe because he went to day care in the UK, and we (I) wanted to keep some sort of routine for him. Was it because I presumed that John would have all his time taken up with job hunting and then working once having secured a job. Yes, that was it. I thought John would just walk into a job and everything had to be good to go to accommodate this.

Our second week, the girls started school. The local intermediate which covered the two years between junior school and college, years 7 and 8, ages 10–12. Lily would be there for nearly two years, and Edie for part of one. It was a shock to their systems with much more freedom and far less control. Less focus on academia, another shock after the UK's approach of rigorous, continuous testing and academic expectation. Less or no homework at all it would seem. Afterall, who needs to work after a day's work right. We all need time to just be, to explore, to be free. A great approach I thought. A well balanced, rounded approach, work/life balance, not just for us adults but for the children too. Just what they both needed. A chance for them both to shine. New Zealand does that so well. Encouraging you to discover your own unique gifts and talents and place in the world. If I had to prefer a system, and I'm not a systems fan, it would be the New Zealand one.

Walker joined kindy, just a few days a week at first whilst John job hunted. After settling in, he loved it. He spent all day outside, come rain or shine. He could be encouraged in for food but was largely outside with his new gang of mates: digging, climbing, playing in puddles. If there was no rain, they had water play. One spare change of clothes was often not enough, but he didn't care. The doors were open, and the children could come and go as they pleased. So far removed from UK childcare setting. Bliss.

I started work. The lovely, retired osteopath greeted me and showed me to my clinic space. It had a direct view of the side of a building, but if you positioned the furniture just so, your eyes were taken to the cathedral and the hills beyond the city. Beautiful.

The clinic itself had a stagnant feel. The energy felt quite heavy although everything seemed to run along just so. Change was not a frequent or regular visitor, and I think I shook the place up a little. I was impatient to get going and make my mark. I was vibrant and full of beans, a loud energy in a sea of beige, my midline still oscillating wildly.

I was shown the computerised clinic diary, not complicated, it was the same Australian software I had used in the UK. We had a lovely receptionist who organised all of our diaries and shouldered a lot of the day-to-day stresses of running busy patient lists. It was a smooth transition actually.

Accident Compensation Corporation (ACC), the Kiwi state health insurance scheme, was a different kettle of fish, however, and took longer to get my head around. I was thrown in at the deep end and had to master it for myself. Where was Alf, my new employer, you might ask? Well, he was in Australia on vacation. Impeccable timing, but he and his lovely wife Karen were well deserving of a break after the trials and tribulations of the visa process. I remain grateful to the other osteopaths. Although they had busy lists and no obligation to help, they frequently went out of their way to do so when I managed to collar them between patients.

I do not think any of the therapists had ever painted their clinic spaces, but I painted mine twice in the relatively short time I was there. Colours chosen for my energetic needs of the moment. The first was darker and womb like, cocooning and protecting after the insanity of the visa process and the intensity of the move. My energy imbibed into the very fabric of the building. Working my hands on the good people of Nelson calmed my midline. I landed, at last, in the present. I was grounding and connecting. Expanding.

The second time I painted it was light, bright, flying, and free. My strong midline now anchoring me in this space, my healing energy free to roam the wider community.

We had landed on the 3rd March 2020. I had started work on the 10th of March 2020. Two weeks later, the 25th of March 2020, just three weeks after arriving in New Zealand, the whole country went into lockdown. Holy shit. I hadn't seen that coming. I'm not sure many did.

That wasn't the worst of it for us. Little did we know at the time that we would not see Gary, the girls would not see their dad, for nearly two and half years.

Chapter 21

That first lockdown was a blessing, other than becoming addicted to the now switched on TV and other devices. We were so exhausted from our move; we were grateful to just stop, albeit by force. As it transpired, we also had the famous virus.

I remember being at work as we were given a short time to prepare for lockdown. Walking up the clinic stairs was making me breathless. I thought I was very unfit. I thought I was very stressed. I thought I was anxious. I probably was all of these things, but what I didn't think I was, was virus riddled.

Towards the end of the first week of lockdown, during an intimate moment, I found myself to be extraordinarily breathless and not in a good way. That was the first real inkling. Then, I was cooking a Sunday roast and realised I couldn't smell it at all. That was the second real sign. Plus, my head felt like it was being crushed under the weight of my dreadlocks, and I enquired if John might cut them off.

Luckily, John was still (and remained) of his right mind and commented, "I don't think it's your dreadlocks, dear. I think you have the lurgy."

Bugger, of course I did, and off to bed I went for the next three days. Headache, fever, loss of smell, body aches, and I was done. The rest of the family passed through without a hitch, they showed symptoms but did not have to take to their beds. As I was perpetually comprising a sympathetic state, relentlessly driven by fight and flight, it was unsurprising that I suffered (relatively) the most.

I took advantage of the time on my hands and completed the child and adolescent training required of me for NZ registration. One hundred hours with the Ara Institute of Canterbury. We were given a few years to complete them. I was grateful to get it out of the way within a few weeks and grateful that it gave me some focus during the strange time we were all experiencing.

We focused on daily routines, mealtimes, exercise. The once a week, one person shop became an adventure. Waiting to see what John would return with became the highlight of the week. The sun shone: we enjoyed yoga on the deck, made paddling pools out of buckets, drew on the sidewalk in chalk, and enjoyed our daily walk around the neighbourhood.

We took to the Nelson hills with a vengeance. We would pack up food for the day and walk kilometres in the wilderness beyond. Oh, the joy of being able to leave your home by foot and fifteen minutes later be teetering on the edge of authentic wilderness was intoxicating.

The energy of the mountains was magnetic and vast. The surge of power was exhilarating. I could feel the magic there, old dragon magic. The energy that came through me was magnified, filling my crown and surging through my hands and feet with such intensity. I have never felt such a connection to a land before. I was upgrading at speed. Ascension as a rite of passage. I had come home.

⇝ ★ ⇜

After the initial lockdown, New Zealand enjoyed a period of calm whilst the rest of the world struggled on. We felt blessed to be here. I had returned to work as soon as possible; where there was a need, I would be of service. The rest of my colleagues followed shortly after, and I finally got to see my new boss, Alf, at work, some three months after arriving.

I was doubly grateful to be back at work. Lockdown had eaten into the savings that we had arrived with. Savings that were intended to buy a yurt to live in. John was still not working, what with it being quite tough to seek employment in a new country during a pandemic lockdown. Plus, we needed to return our temporary accommodation to its owner. It was the right thing to do. They, too, had been impacted. Due to the border closure, they could not leave New Zealand for their planned foreign travel. We needed to find somewhere else to live and trying to negotiate yurt living with the council was proving problematic. We ended up in a lovely old house on a busy road right in the centre of town. Far removed from our idea of rural yurt living. The house spoke to me though. The Universe said this is the house, so we took it, even if it was the opposite of what we (I) thought we wanted.

The toll on our finances was so severe that I had to declare myself bankrupt during that lockdown. Extraordinarily intimidating and stressful, and I would be left breathless with anxiety trying to deal with debtors in the UK. We had come on a wing and a prayer, and everything had hinged on John getting work as soon as we landed. I (we) hadn't factored in a global pandemic. Everything had been done hand to mouth. Selling our limited worldly possessions just to get the flights, etc. I was so grateful to have my job security and the pandemic aid offered by New Zealand.

Work was busy, and as the new practitioner, my case load was soon filled with a variety of patients, some of which were not suited to me and my style of treating. Not to worry, the energy would soon settle and those that would benefit from my vibration would sort themselves. We are not suited to everyone, and everyone is not suited to us at any given time. That is simple energetics, and I have learned that life is easier when you lovingly accept this.

I have also learned that the more of yourself you are able to heal, the more you are able to help heal in others. The power coming through is magnified. Healer heal thyself, I think we have all heard the saying. There is one thing to hear the saying and quite another to experience it. When I experience a levelling up of my energetic system, the patients benefit tenfold. It's like having new superpowers. Quite extraordinary.

Chapter 22

Back when I was still in junior school, aged 10 or so, we went on a school camping trip. I learned something on that trip that wounded me so deeply it inadvertently became a major fulcrum of my own life path. It was so massive to me that every decision I made from that day on was influenced by my newfound knowledge. I won't talk too much on it here, only to say that my foundation in life was shaken to the core. That deep sense of knowing who I was and where I belonged, my place in the world was shattered. To have absolutely no knowledge of what I was being told, the truth of who I was, who I thought I was, taken from me.

Something otherworldly entered me that day. It sat right at my solar plexus. It was small, the size of a tennis ball, dense and dark with short sharp spikes. Unbeknownst to me at this time, it began feeding from the light of my solar plexus, knocking my solar plexus, commonly thought of as the family centre, off balance.

The light we emit from our seven main energy centres (chakras) must remain in balanced harmony otherwise dis-ease will set in the physical body and our mental and emotional fields deregulate. The seven largest and most widely known are found at your crown, your third eye (forehead), your throat, your heart, your solar plexus, your abdomen, and your sacral root (base).

The energy of the solar plexus, between your naval (belly button) and the bottom of your sternum, governs your confidence, sense of self and direction in life. When out of balance, low self-esteem and control issues prevail. My downward spiral started with this newfound knowledge and subsequent dysregulation of my solar plexus, and it would take me on quite a journey over the next two decades.

In time I will write this journey. I must for my own healing journey and spiritual expansion to continue, but for the moment we remain here with my osteopathic odyssey.

With my decision to study osteopathy back in 2010, I had unwittingly taken my first true step upon my healing path. It was a transitionary point at which I truly began to learn to love myself. Where I began to find my place in the world and even if I did not know it then, I had begun my journey back to wholeness.

The healing journey can be a turbulent affair. Up and down, round and round we plod on, painful at times but ever moving forward, even if it doesn't feel like it at times. You've just got to keep doing the work. The work on yourself. It can feel beyond frustrating and that in itself is a lesson.

My solar plexus frustrated me. I was experiencing all these magical moments but felt stuck in myself right at my horizontal and vertical midline, where all planes of magic radiate from. I had to overcome frustration, impatience, and ego that I could not shift this little black spikey beast that weighed so heavily upon me. It would catch me unawares, and I could feel its presence, a darkness in my light.

I knew deep down though, when the time was right, it would shift. I just had to trust. So, me and my little spiky pal went about our business until I landed in Nelson. Then it was countdown to eviction.

※ ★ ※

After everything we had (collectively) been through, I needed a treatment. I didn't want to take liberties with my colleague's time, so I booked myself in properly for a sound healing with a lovely lady who also worked with us. Sound healing works with vibration. It resonates through us, clearing stuck energy in our physical bodies and energetic debris from our etheric fields. When Alf found out I was seeking treatment, he also offered to treat me. Happy days. A blissful sound healing followed by a biodynamic osteopathic treatment; this was going to be good.

I'd never had a sound healing before. Beyond my training, I did not go out of my way to ask for help from others, ever. Even to book and pay for it was alien to me to believe that I was worthy of healing help. Prior to training, I had never experienced for myself any healing therapy. For me, my saviour and solace had always been alcohol.

During the sound healing, a large, crystal bowl was placed upon my solar plexus. The lovely Marianne intuitively guided to my area of need, she began to rub the rim, round and round, coaxing the beautiful bowl to sing. The vibration of the sound was incredible. The feeling as it reverberated through my physical, emotional, and mental fields and out into the spiritual space beyond – what a beautiful experience. I could feel my little pal rattling around, getting agitated, all shook up. Interesting.

As soon as my sound healing had finished, I made my way to Alf's room. I laid on my back on his treatment couch. He placed his hands at the back of my head, gently cradling my cranium, and we settled into the treatment. Alf working as a channel for divine light to enter my system. The barriers between us disappeared, and light filled us both.

Now, I am blessed with the ability to feel and see beyond the obvious range. We all have latent abilities, we are just at different points of our journey. I am by no means unique, but it is truly awesome when you find and can work with another sensitive person. What a gift for me Alf was right then. We really do need others even if we think we don't.

No sooner had Alf started, then my little spiky pal began to shift. His ferocious grip had been loosened by the divine sound healing. While Alf worked, he shook and shifted from my solar plexus right up through my oesophagus and out of my mouth, making me convulse and gag in the process.

"Bloody hell, Alf! Did you see that?"

Yes, he did.

Holy Mackerel. That right there was a bloody miracle. I literally could not believe it. It had finally shifted after all this time. It had been in there for three decades.

I felt a bit rough after those two divine sessions, which is not unusual when you have a massive energetic shift. Rather unfairly, the feeling can be similar to that of a hangover, and I hadn't been drunk in a good while now. A toxic dump is a toxic dump though, and the feelings on the system are the same. I went home to drink lots of water, rest (try to), and integrate the spectacular shift.

It can feel slightly discombobulating to lose something that has influenced you for so long. I wasn't sad to see him go though, only excited for what lay ahead. What else could be achieved without the input of that troublesome little blighter.

You know what else shifted that day? Aside from the incredible skill of my colleagues with their beautiful healing modalities and unique vibration, it was the simple fact that I had finally learned to ask for help. Something that I should have done a long time ago.

The magic did not stop there. That was not the culmination of all.

My angel wings stemmed from my cervical dorsal junction, where the base of your neck meets the top of your back and continued down my thoracic spine between my scapulae. Very large, very beautiful, made up of long white feathers. Of course, it was logical that there would be another pair at the next junction, the dorsal lumbar junction, edging down my lumbar spine. My sparkly, colourful, translucent fae set. Smaller but just as beautiful. That made sense. Nice and orderly. I like that.

We have of course another major junction. The lumbar sacral junction, where the lumbar spine meets the sacrum. Second guessing the Universe was (is) futile, and I was happy to wait and see.

I began to glimpse the dragons. When I was working, I often saw the triangular tip of a dragon tail flicking out of sight. Out walking the hills I could feel the strong pull through the ground. Pathways and patterns of a strong energy becoming clearer. The dragon's breath resting in the surrounding hills and mountains. The dragons were here.

I'm sure you can guess what happened next ...

It was not long before I was gifted my very own set of small black dragon wings. Right at the bottom of my spine. Perfectly neat, leathery, and deepest black. They popped out during another work session, this time here in Nelson. The energy of my root recognising the strong connection to the earth beneath my feet, grounding me here in this place. New Zealand.

⇃ ★ ⇂

After my glorious sessions resulting in the removal of my spiky pal, the world of self-care really opened to me. I could truly see and feel the benefits of asking for help, joining with others instead of living on the fringes and flying solo as I had for so long. I felt the pull to keep my energy fields clear, to maintain my wings, to find my tribe, my community.

I began attending plant medicine ceremonies. Cacao was my first and opened my heart. I drove out of Nelson, over Takaka Hill, which feels as if it will never end; higher and higher you go, leaving the valley floor far behind before dropping down into the calm and tranquillity of Golden Bay with its lush green valleys and stunning bays. It was a perfect backdrop to my first ever ceremonial event.

I had the most surreal experience the first time I attended to dance with cacao on a full moon. We started sat in a quiet circle, maybe twenty of us, a meditation to ground us in the space and the drinking of the ceremonial cacao, hot, spicy, viscous, and deeply earthy. And then we danced, silence apart from the earthy beat of the tunes coming from the most resplendent DJ booth, decks spun by the most beautiful space holding ethereal goddess, Katyayani. The tunes were alive and wove their way through me, moving me, lifting me.

I felt the spirit of Mumma Cacao enter me, beautiful red and gold. My body moved in ways I could not conceive; I was not in control. I lost all concept of time. A time came, and it was late, I collapsed on a bench on my back. I felt my liver vibrate and my gall bladder squirt. My system was flooded with toxic overload, and I felt simultaneously very drunk and very hung over. There was no way I could drive back over the hill. I needed to eat and then I needed to sleep. I slept in my van in the car park and drove back the next day.

"Are you telling me you got high on hot chocolate?" John enquired as I arrived home a day late.

Not quite high from the cacao itself, I explained, but Mumma Cacao released from me a load that I had been carrying that I no longer needed. Subsequently, my system overloaded for a short time whilst it assimilated and flushed through, such was the load it had been carrying. Poor liver. The liver is known to carry your unassimilated or expressed anger. I had been such an angry teenager. What a gift to be able to work through this now and in such a magical way.

Each time you make these tangible shifts, it is hard to explain the new knowing and profound gratitude to be able to move through mental and emotional challenges that are holding you back. Especially when you reach a place where you can understand on a deep level the need to move through them. Your awareness accelerates. The need to keep flowing and shifting. The changes afterwards, thought patterns and energetic ties to people and places, to situations and events. Your perception shifts and you expand further.

I frequented more sound healings, laying silently with others, supported by pillows and blankets whilst divine beings played crystal bowls, chimes, gongs, didgeridoo, or any manner of other powerful musical taonga. Powerful spiritual objects creating waves of change through my system.

I enjoyed attending Blue Lotus tea ceremonies, which were frequently held prior to a particular crystal bowl sound healings. They were most enlightening. Blue Lotus sure does clear and activate your third eye. It tingles like crazy as your spiritual vision clears, amplifying the deep truths we all hold within.

I also engaged with some amazing, distant healing. I was completely blown away. A wonderful duo in Auckland work with ascended masters for ascension in this lifetime. I sent them a photo of myself, and at the predetermined time, I lay on my bed and waited. I did not have to wait long. I could feel them coming.

Healing with ascended masters, those that have walked this Earth before just like you and me and have had lifetimes of toil and trauma just like you and me. The difference being they have completed the lessons needed to clear their karmic debt, and they have ascended. Familiar beings such as Jesus, Mother Mary, Mary Magdalene, Ganesh, Lao Tze among many others.

I could feel them working. Pushing and pulling, through my physical body and etheric fields. Clearing the debris of accumulated lifetimes and filling my whole being with light. The greatest gift they have given me was clearing a strong-rooted blockage deep in my mind that was prohibiting me from carrying out my own distant healings. It was held right at my pineal gland. A contract from a past life prohibiting me to use my gifts in such a way. A remnant from a time when using one's gifts was dangerous for the fear it instilled in others. The blockage popped out like a visceral cork from a bottle, and I instantaneously knew I would be able to perform distant healings from this moment on. The bind to my past contract was broken. Time and space was no longer a barrier to healing. With this new release emerged a new divine helper, an oriental looking whirling dervish, much like a sufi. He carries with him a powerful staff and pops out of my crown when I work to heal distant lands and spaces. He spins and spins and bangs his staff on the ground sending shock waves through the horizontal plane, clearing lifetimes of trauma and energetic debris. Gratitude.

Chapter 23

My treatment room continued to be a crowded affair. I frequently noticed the front row spectators, who were not merely spectators but active participants. A Hollywood lookalike, a balding monk, a faceless, gliding apparition and a blue grey alien who appears to carry out psychic surgery. Whoever you are, kudos and gratitude that you choose to work through this perfectly imperfect channel.

    The power of the Universe coming through was outrageous. The tangibility of the energy was exponentially increasing. The more I embraced it, the easier it became. By embrace I mean truly settle into it. Since my days of qualification, I had yearned to embrace the spiritual aspect of osteopathy whole heartedly, but something held me back. That something I now see was the fear of others. The fear of how others may perceive me. If you know me, this may come somewhat as a surprise. Some little fearful niggle held me back from taking that final leap of embrace. This was compounded by the other fear of others, the unspoken fears others have of discussing spirituality within our work. The perceived need to fit into a mainstream narrative. Fortunately, those that approach osteopathy are not usually seeking the mainstream narrative.

Spiritual healing is a vital part of our healing of the whole. Let us not forget the number one principle of osteopathy: We are a unit: body, mind, and spirit. With my qualification I had mastered, to some extent (always that of a beginner in the eyes of the Universe), the physical body, and I certainly had the ability to be of service within the spiritual realm, so why shouldn't I? Why should I not proudly offer this service. The Universe had shown me how to use these parts of myself, and I should most definitely honour the Universe by doing so.

I began to set myself apart from my colleagues in terms of treatment style. I had always been a little left of centre anyway. People that needed what I could offer found their way to me. I continued to focus mainly on the body and all its constituents: muscle, bone, ligaments, tendons, organs, blood, lymph, cerebral spinal fluid, nerves, arteries, veins, you get the picture. On top of that, with chronic patients initially, those that struggled to attain change, I would offer to check their energetic system. It would not take me long and certainly would not hurt; such was my skill.

When you work with energy often, it becomes easier to feel and a natural extension of yourself. I have sat with this for a long time and it is as natural to me as breathing. It is the breath of life after all, and I feel it moving through me. In and out, in and out. An orchestra of breath. Nonstop. Infinite. The breath of the Universe.

Where I had always been able to effectively "floss" the energy centres using my hands, I could clearly feel the persons energy blockages in myself. I began to move more in treatment, fluid, gliding movements beyond my control as the energy moved between us, clearing, cleansing, and expanding. The humble burp and blow remaining an ever-efficient way to clear oneself during treatment. Either of us able to ground or clear the energetic debris or attachments through our feet or expel to the Universe through our crowns. These decisions never mine to make, what occurs is what needs to, part of the process and wholly organic in nature. You lay peacefully whilst I move around you, not connecting with your physical body but working in the space beyond. An open channel of divine light.

As I pass my hands over the major energy centres, I can feel whether they are blocked with no movement, whether they are spinning erratically or are generally sluggish. Where they are very stuck, my hand is magnetised to them. It takes all my strength to refrain from contacting the body. In these cases, there is often something outside of ourselves blocking the channel and that something needs removing. This can be fun.

One such time, the removal came with such force I was thrown against the clinic wall, other times where I have been seated on my wheely stool, I have been wheeled across the floor. Sometimes these attachments can be noisy or attempt to appear scary. I let them know I "see" them, and they are whooshed away by whatever means are appropriate through feet or crown.

Common areas for attachments are the throat and heart, followed by the solar plexus. The throat commonly for women of a certain age, for they have long held their tongue in a bid to keep the peace. The heart, who of us through our lifetimes have not been heart wounded? The solar plexus relates to our family and who amongst us can claim a fully functional "normal" family. What even is that? Families by their very nature are designed to teach us some of our toughest lessons. These areas are prone to hurt, and where we are wounded our light leaks out. Where our light leaks out is where we become a beacon for Other. Some people refer to Other as entities. Energies from other places.

This Other can sit with you a long time, sometimes a lifetime. Just as one sat at my solar plexus. Sometimes it sits on your shoulder whispering in your ear, downplaying your emotional and mental capabilities. The proverbial chip on your shoulder.

A favourite patient was a lady who attended for menopause issues. As treatment progressed, we naturally moved onto her energy field. As I began to work around her head, throat, and heart, I could feel a strong presence on her left shoulder. I was overcome with feelings of inadequacy. I wondered what on earth I was doing, I had no right or qualification to do what I was doing, what would people think of me? How dare I! I should stop, and for a moment I believed that true of myself.

Fortunately, I swiftly realised that this was not mine. But for that moment it was the strongest sensation, the strongest influence of Other upon myself, of another's Other that I have ever felt. For that moment, it completely influenced my belief system, and I felt what my lovely patient had been fighting unwittingly all these years.

I would not have thought this of my patient. She, to the outside world, had been successful in her work life, had a great marriage and family, was affluent and had everything she could possibly need. What was never voiced during treatment was her crushing imposter syndrome. She was an artist and created for family and friends but never felt good enough to put herself out there to a wider audience. When I gave voice to the feelings I was experiencing of hers through the energy healing, it all came out. All the feelings of inadequacy she had carried her whole life. Stemming from something her grandmother would tell her as a child. These feelings continued to haunt her and hold her back through her entire life. As soon as the Other was removed, she approached galleries and began to display her work to great success and was soon taking private commissions and earning money for doing what she truly loved. Would she have achieved that level of healing through body work alone? Who knows.

Another type of clearing is the clearing of energetic congestion that is of Self, and this can result in my burping or blowing as I integrate and dissipate your energetic congestion through my field. I always keep the windows of the clinic open to facilitate the removal of this energetic congestion. Good ventilation is paramount, and you just cannot beat fresh air. This can feel quite nauseating but is not harmful to myself. I am yet to vomit during treatment but recently the feelings are amplifying, and the burps can border on the edge of orgasmic. I am going through another transition of my own so will wait to see the outcome of this. Beneficial for all parties involved no doubt.

And finally, based on my own understanding, the other energy that often needs clearing is the energy of Another. As a pelvic health advocate, this is where I often see this manifest. The frequent result of union with Another. The culmination of two souls coming together and the transfer of energy from one to another. Unfortunately, this is not always a happy union.

A lady attended for pelvic issues, she had split with her husband a few years previously and had not yet found another with whom to share her life. There is a saying: make space and things will come. Clear out the old and make way for the new and this is true for ourselves by being able to release the cords that bind us with Another. Clear their energy from our systems and you will begin to vibrate differently. You will send out different signals and you may well attract what your heart desires. And so it was for this lady after we cleared her sacred space. The very next time I saw her she was in a new relationship, very happy, and excited for the future.

A lovely, elderly lady came in, stiff and sore all over. Treatment progressed well, and she made good physical improvements. Further along though, she was frequently breathless with no obvious cause. I referred her to the doctors and in light of no unusual findings, I asked to look at her energy field.

I was pleasantly surprised; her main centres felt quite clear. I enquired as to her spiritual health care as I had not expected this clarity. She spoke of her religious beliefs and frequency of prayer. Well, that is beautiful, I thought. As I made my way down to her pelvis it became more congested, and she spoke of babies lost not previously mentioned. As I went down her right side, past her feet, and back up the left, I sensed something deeper through her heart. The appearance of clarity was superficial. It was hiding something much deeper and darker.

The treatment turned into quite the battle. A seething mass of dark, black sludge was sitting directly in her heart space, long tendrils wrapping around the heart and lungs. It would not shift without a fight. I magnetised to it. I felt the resistance in myself as I drew him out. It was him. It all came out. How her husband had been hard to live with, a narcissist who eventually committed suicide many years ago. In all our sessions together, this had not been touched upon even though I am probing with my questions, naturally nosey, and always striving to understand the bigger picture.

She went home, promptly vomited, and had a large, drawn out, bowel clearing session. She was so impressed by this, she phoned to tell me all about it. She felt much better. A good purge after this kind of treatment is always a possibility and often indicates the depth of energetic dysfunction.

So, in a nutshell, our energy can be effected, as I have seen it so far, by Other (worldly), Self (own) and Another (human). Our energy system is a vital part of our whole and requires attention when we seek profound and deep healing for ourselves. Simple really.

How can you begin to integrate healing on your own path? Physically, mentally, emotionally and spiritually. It really is as simple as starting to look at what you fuel your body with, your nutrition. Eat more whole foods and less processed food. Stop filling yourself with toxic junk that affects you across all levels of your being.

Then look at how you use your body. Do you move enough? Do you have a desk job? Do you make time for movement? Especially movement that takes you away from your midline. Jogging is a midline exercise. Cycling is a midline exercise. Yoga and Pilates take you away from your midline and encourage you to clear the spaces that do not often see the light. You need balance in your life. There is internal exercise, working with your breath and movement in a practice such as Tai Chi or Bagua, an internal martial art. Are you even breathing properly? You can look at a practice involving stillness such as chakra meditation or mindfulness to begin to address the energy field specifically. Walking in nature, swimming in natural bodies of water, and walking barefoot on the ground. Feel the connection to the very earth that sustains us and the universe beyond. Nature clears us; we are symbiotic with nature.

Take a good look at a typical day in your life. Are you content? Are you peaceful? Are you kind to yourself and others? Think about how you talk to yourself or others, be mindful of what you say. Words carry energy and are powerful. Are there situations that you need to address for a change that befits your higher self? Do you feel stuck in a rut? Make a change! Pick just one thing to instigate a cascade of positive change in your life.

Then begin to consider life events that have caused you pain or trauma. Have you transmuted these or are they still present in your system? Do they still cause emotional upset or dictate the way you see, speak, or behave repetitive obstructive painful loops of thoughts and feelings. Who can help you other than yourself?

Change comes from within, but there are some very inciteful tools at your disposal to aid your transformation: physical therapists, talking therapists, energy healers, nutritionists, homeopaths, and of course osteopaths to name only a very few. The diversity in the healing space is incredible. There is so much choice and opportunity. Slow down enough to listen to your internal voice, go where your intuition guides you. If someone resonates with you, go and see them. You too can begin to experience contentment and peace. Harmony in the flow of life is yours for creating. You are a divine creatrix. Get creating.

Chapter 24

Our first year here ticked by. Our plan of having Gary come every six months had been blown to smithereens. Chaos was ensuing at home in Nelson. The New Zealand government closed the border shortly after our arrival in March 2020 and it had remained closed. Gary had been due to arrive six weeks after us. As we had all lived together prior to leaving for New Zealand, it was understandably very upsetting for the girls that they would not be seeing their dad as quickly as we had hoped. We tried to keep their morale up. It was tough; they were very brave girls. We kept reassuring them that they would see their dad soon, but who of us really knew?

I was kept preoccupied with completing my competent authority pathway program (CAPP). This is a yearlong program that has to be completed by all osteopaths from abroad wishing to work in New Zealand. The program is overseen by a preceptor chosen for you from several experienced osteopathic practitioners willing to take up the role of the yearlong supervision required. I was late starting it due to the first lockdown but got into it when we were able to return to work. It involved many case studies, liaising with other health professionals, setting goals and actioning them, researching the New Zealand health system and writing up reports. It was drawn out and time consuming. Tough when you are trying to earn money and settle into a new country, especially during a pandemic. I finished my CAPP program around July of 2021, a month or so shy of my year deadline. I had fantastic feedback, scoring highly throughout. New Zealand was happy to have me here.

I did not see what was coming.

During August 2021 we experienced what was to be our final lockdown due to the pandemic here in Nelson. Our largest city, Auckland, had it much harder and longer than the rest of New Zealand. It is all relative, and we all have our stories to tell. For me, the "ease" of the initial lockdown where we experienced the virus, went bankrupt, studied, ate lovely food, enjoyed long walks in the surrounding countryside, and long lazy days of yoga and reading, was replaced by a palpable fear that our lives were being restricted in such a way that our spirits were being crushed. I began to drink again.

Fast forward a few months to October 2021 and the government mandated the New Zealand health sector. A large portion of the New Zealand health workforce, including myself, would be mandated to take a pharmaceutical intervention to keep their jobs. Other sectors were also mandated but the timelines varied. Also, to partake freely in society moving forward, you would need a verified pass.

Our world imploded. I, along with many others, would have to leave their jobs. I would no longer have the "right" to call myself an osteopath. We would no longer be able to move freely around town. We were limited to essential food/medical shopping. No clubs, cafes, restaurants. No non-essential physical shopping. No admittance to cinemas, swimming pools, the theatre, fairs, fetes, water parks, animal parks, theme parks, the list goes on.

The health mandates came into effect in November 2021, and the passes followed shortly at the end of school term, early December 2021. Just in time for summer break and Christmas festivities.

Before school ended for the year, Lily got to attend the outdoor swim slides as a school group. An end of school year celebration. The very next weekend, the start of the summer break, she was refused access on her birthday as she had no pass. It had started. She was devastated. A crying young girl in her bikini on the street on her birthday. A truly sad sight. Her friends corralled her. We put our heads together. Passes were for aged 12 and a quarter and over. We juggled her birth date and in they went.

No more gym classes for Lily should she care to return, and pottery class was cancelled for Edie. I fought hard for Edie to remain in her pottery class. Her mental health was fast deteriorating due to being kept apart from her dad and this one thing kept her buoyant during those turbulent times. With sound reasoning on my part, she was allowed to remain, but the decision was not without collateral damage. She endured the pain of being initially excluded, and I lost good friends in the fight for her ultimate inclusion. I hadn't made many friends, we had only been here a short while, but the couple of good ones that I had made did not have the foundation of years of solid friendship to hold up the relationship in the wake of differing viewpoints.

The girls had already suffered at school and that was to spill over into the holidays, into what should have been a time of respite. Fear drove others to truly heinous reasoning. Our girls were told that their parents did not care for them and that we would all die. It was hard enough to fit in and make friends during a pandemic when routine of school was so often disrupted. Add to that the non-conformity to societal norms of the times and you find yourself with two very upset teenagers. We bolstered them, proud of their resilience and strength in the face of adversity. We have always encouraged the girls to make their own choices based on what feels right and true for them, the only source of truth their own, and we took the same view here. I was thankful they chose to walk this path with us, and we encouraged them to seek out others with similar viewpoints whilst the situation remained contentious. Thankfully, where there is darkness, there is light, and this was a time for ingenuity. It is during tough times though that the greatest learnings are achieved, and teenagers are resilient and resourceful. They found ways to get to where they needed to be. They found friends to support them and help them in their adventurous endeavours over summer.

We were supposed to be looking forward to a boring long summer with no access to our favourite places. I had always taught the girls that when the going gets tough, go for a long walk. We had been booked to walk the Heaphy Track as a family, a 78km trail of wholesome, healing goodness. Great for the soul. We would be carrying our own food and all of our own camping equipment, and we would remain well out of anyone's way. Unfortunately, as it transpired, we had no pass; therefore, we were not allowed access to these monitored wilds, and our hike was cancelled. I would have taken the challenge if I were a solo traveller, but I had my family to consider and did not want our children to feel any more ostracised than they already did.

This only served to fan my enthusiasm though, and we tramped further into the wilds on tracks less travelled, in places where we did not need permission or a pass. Great healing is found in nature, and we would not be deprived of it. Lily and I tramped the Inland

Pack Track, a multiday wilderness adventure on the wild West Coast which entailed walking the riverbeds through towering limestone canyons.

At times we had to wade through chest deep water with our packs held over our heads, having to be mindful that if there were to be a deluge and the rivers rose, exit points were few and far between. We freedom camped at beautiful swim holes we were guided to by the animal tracks along the river. Memories of lazing on pristine, white sandy riverbanks and bathing in crystal clear waters, being watched over by the mountain spirits all around, filled us. We pitched our tent when and where we wanted, not another soul in sight for days on end. Fell asleep to fiery sunsets, waking to misty mornings with only the sound of native birds, crickets and cicadas to break the wide silence. Camping in an expansive limestone outcrop known as the Ballroom Overhang found at the confluence of the Fox River and Dilemma Creek as we made our way out was a highlight of the summer and the first time we saw another person. Climbing high up the canyon only to find a fresh landslip with huge drop offs got the heart racing, especially when we met rangers coming in to assess the recent slip as we neared civilisation once more. We were proud to have navigated these obstacles by ourselves. What a metaphor for life in troubled times. An exhilarating adventure. These memories will remain with me forever. What a gift our exclusion had brought us.

In hindsight, what actually transpired was a beautiful summer spent meeting beautiful people in far flung areas of New Zealand that we might not have travelled to had this situation not arose. Social media, for all its woes, became the place to connect with others in our situation. We became a different kind of freedom camper. An interactive map was realised, and it allowed us to drop a pin in where we knew we could find solace and kin with whom we could navigate these turbulent times. There were a lot of pins in that map as more and more people added to it. A freedom community was born, and it was beautiful. We spent the summer exploring the East Coast then traversing mountainous passes to reach the West Coast before heading home. Along the way, we connected with people who did not hold with the pass system, who welcomed us with open arms and wide smiles. People who put on activities for us and the children, who fed us, and entertained us. I will forever remember those people with gratitude. The ability to shine their light through trying times is divinity in action indeed.

Chapter 25

The introduction of the mandates alongside the verified passes meant I had to rethink my working environment. From the outset, we had two weeks to comply. Those two weeks were spent working, drinking, and raging.

Fortunately, the powers that be saw fit to extend the deadline by a further two weeks, a little grace as I worked to pack up my professional life as I knew it just before the long school summer break which also coincides with Christmas in the Southern Hemisphere. Gratefully, I got myself together. You can only rage so much before action must be taken to move forward. That was the situation and we had to deal with it. I had to deal with it. Giving myself completely over to alcohol, no matter how appealing it seemed at the time was not an option. I roped in everyone I could, namely John, Alf, and the kids, into a monumental project. I had a plan.

When we had moved into our Universe decreed rental, it had in its past had a room under the house that had been removed during the restoration. John and I, over the previous year, had lovingly reinstated it and it was a sanctuary outside of the house for our eldest, Edie. It had its own access and entrance separate from the main house.

Edie was to give up her sanctuary as part of the great plan. To compensate her for her gracious exit, John and I gave up the master bedroom in the house. She was left quite satisfied by this arrangement. Now John and I had nowhere to sleep. Ah, not to worry, I had that covered.

At the top of our sloping section, directly outside of the kitchen, above the outside sanctuary, was a gnarly, sloping, wet area. This area we decked. Deep holes were dug, perfectly as John was the executioner of these, and he is a perfectionist. Posts were erected and a large, flat deck area was created, helped hugely by the wonderful Alf who, alongside his professional family, had also chosen to walk the same path as us. On this large flat area, we erected a canvas bell tent. This was to be John's and my bedroom for as long as necessary.

I felt truly triumphant and jubilant. I had wanted to live outside for so long, and now I was getting exactly what I wanted with the amenities of a house right next door. Winning once more. Luckily John was happy too. He's not called "Easy John" for nothing. He shares my great love for the natural world and will always jump at the chance to connect with it at ever deeper levels.

The outside sanctuary just needed a quick wipe down and brush over with a fresh coat of paint. A blind, my favoured koru inspired window decals, and a sumptuous privacy curtain to complete its cosy feel. I arranged for an Eftpos machine to be installed, grateful that the installation technician was also following the same path. Finally, I hung a Turkish glass evil eye, gifted to me by my mother years ago, above the door to protect me from prying eyes and we were good to go. My new workspace was born. A grand effort over two weeks.

At the end of our crazy busy two weeks grace, Alf and I, along with others, bid farewell to our colleagues and left the central city clinic where I had worked since landing in New Zealand and of which Alf was a founding, longstanding member. The reliable source of our livelihoods gone in a flash.

I was so grateful that we were already residents here in New Zealand, if I had been on a work visa, as some of my colleagues were, I would have had to return home to the UK, my family in tow. As it was, I was by now a self-employed osteopath having been working alongside Alf instead of for him for the last eight months. I would just have to be a self-employed something else now.

To all intents and purposes, I was no longer allowed to refer to myself as an osteopath. Fortunately, my identity is not tied up to the fact that I was (am) an osteopath. I could see a path forward where some of my colleagues couldn't. I was still Kelly. I held a bachelor's degree in osteopathy and a postgraduate diploma in women's health. I knew there would still be a large portion of our community that needed me and my skills, and so I put my healer hat on.

Kelly the healer shifted her work life from the large clinic in town seamlessly into the sanctuary in her garden, and without giving space to draw breath, quietly and conscientiously continued to work.

People came as I knew they would. I was no longer registered as an osteopath and could not provide the ACC cover that people of New Zealand are fortunate to access. Still, they came. People that followed me from town. People that felt that they had nowhere else to go. People who felt that no one would see them or listen to their stories. All different kinds of people. They knew they had a safe space with me, so they came.

I continued to hold that space, welcoming people into our home for more than a year and a half whilst John and I slept a full year outside until our tent succumbed to the ravages of a very wet year. It still saddens me that the tent ended up down the tip. She had been erected under a magnificent magnolia tree which had dropped sap and attracted mould that had eaten its way into her. In a bid to clean and reseal her, which took away her ethereal natural cotton feel, I inadvertently turned her into a sieve.

I truly loved my time in her. In the depths of winter, I would be fully clothed with my hat and gloves on whilst John slept in his underwear and a t-shirt. He only ever put trousers on once and that was when he was poorly. When our lovely tent failed, we slept for months on a mattress in the front room so that I could continue to treat from the room outside. We eventually reshuffled the house so that I ended up treating from the front room and Edie reclaimed her space outside. It would be a while yet until I felt comfortable enough or was even allowed to take my business back into town.

How I missed the bell tent though. I loved the fact that we could be warm outside, under the stars, in winter. Nothing can beat nightly star gazing, the tangible proximity to the weather and the sound and snuffles of local wildlife. Our year outside … heaven. What a gift our exclusion had brought us.

Chapter 26

During the days of the mandates, I did continue to drink, albeit mostly in moderation.

"It's okay, I got this," I told myself.

The limitations imposed resulted in an inability to access any osteopathic continued professional development (CPD) as I was no longer a registered osteopath, and I looked beyond the scope of osteopathy to expand my knowledge base and work on my personal growth. Another blessing in disguise.

With our recent osteopathic conference in Queenstown cancelled due to the August 2021 lockdown I looked to engage with a teaching that could not be cancelled or taken away from me without notice. I felt the need for security, the ability to see something through under my own steam with no interference from outside sources.

I would have preferred to work directly with a teacher but in this instance, I looked for an online platform that could deepen my learning in shamanism. I came across Medicine Woman Centre for Shamanic and Esoteric Studies based in New Zealand who offered a range of metaphysical courses working with teacher plants of New Zealand. The spirits of the native flora of New Zealand.

The House of the Bee Mystery School as it was known, drew me in. I ummed and ahhed for a while. It was a lot of money and a leap of faith was needed to partake in an online school. This is when the bees began to show up. In conversation, in pillows, honey, and face cream gifted to me, I became obsessed with the multitude of honeybees who graced the borage in our garden and would sit and commune with them daily and finally with one big fuzzy bumble bee bumbling right into my sanctuary and bumping me repeatedly.

"Go on, go on," he said.

"Okay, okay," I replied. "I will sign up."

On the next new moon, I signed up for the two-year shamanic studies course. The money was paid, and I felt excited as I waited for my first 24 light flower essences of New Zealand to show up. These wise teacher plants would guide me on my journey as I acquired powerful professional skills to enable me to facilitate rapid transformation, deep soul and spiritual healing, and extraordinary change for myself and others. It promised to enable me to fulfil my unique destiny and be of greater service to others and the planet. Myself, others, the entire planet could do with that right now. What an exciting way to be of service to myself and the Universe.

"Bring it on," I told the bees.

You want to change the world, folks? Well, you've got to start with yourself. This course turbo boosted the process for me. When all around was chaos, I went within. I loved it from the beginning. Being super sensitive and able to feel the vibration of the individual teacher plants was exciting. I had never partaken in any ritual practice except maybe the Ouija board as a youth. Does that count?

We used to set it up in a ram shackle, dilapidated old house by the woods in the village and once in the toilets of the local youth club. It was slightly terrifying, and we all fled the youth club with a friend breaking a bone on the way out. A subsequent grounding for me by my mother. I was not to dabble in the dark arts she told me. Lesson learned.

This was not the dark arts though. Far from it. Light all the way, baby. I loved the ceremony and ritual aspect. The first time I set up my altar, donned my shamanic shawl and medicine bag, and called the power of the Universe in with my arms raised above my head, I felt right at home. The energy shot through my hands radiating through my heart and third eye and grounding me through my feet to this plane. I was suspended between the upper and lower worlds, and everything else fell away. I was one with the Universe. Light coming in above and flowing out below. I radiated light. I knew I had done this before and it served to further confirm my intuition, my innate knowing, that I had walked this path through many lifetimes.

The studies followed the lunar cycle, imbibing a different teacher plant each cycle. The strength and method changing with the phases of the moon. I became super tuned with the moon, compounded by the fact that I was sleeping outside. Under the star lit sky, my menstruation aligned with the powerful full moon, the blood bright and cleansing as it washed away any niggling fears or doubt of our future here in New Zealand. I collected the menstrual blood, diluted it and watered our plants with it. It was a deeply nourishing time connecting to the earth and plants in this sacred ceremonial way.

Nationwide, emotions were running high. In February 2022, inspired by the trucker's convoy in Canada, NZ began their own convoy. I painted up our old van with Walker's bath crayons and joined with them from Nelson to Blenheim. It was a great atmosphere with many in fancy dress with their vehicles decorated. There were many and they were headed to Wellington, the capital of New Zealand in the North Island. The support was overwhelming.

From all corners of the country, ordinary folk were on the move and were gathering together in Wellington, and so began the Freedom Protest. Unable to physically follow them, I followed the protest online until I could no longer contain myself. I jumped on a plane and went to join them for four days where I largely spent my time working with beautiful people in the healing tents.

The folks I met there were ordinary everyday people from all walks of life. Fellow healthcare workers, firemen, farmers, plumbers, electricians, secretary's, chefs, CEOs, lawyers, teachers. The list goes on. A vibrant mix of all ages and ethnicities. People whose lives were being dismantled before their very eyes. People were losing connection to their friends and families, to their homes and jobs. People came to be heard. People came to find connection.

The vibe was high through all attempts to belittle and diminish us. My favourites of all were the Hari Krishnas, and I will forever remember their joyful faces, beautiful music, and nourishing food. The protest was a logistical feat of Kiwi ingenuity built from the kindness and generosity of the people.

My personal path to addiction was loss of connection with an inability to cope and process my emotions. Now society was attempting to suppress them for me. We were not being heard. I was not being heard. I suppressed my emotions and carried on in my usual strong and positive way. I was on shaky ground.

I carried on working from home. The colourful writing on my van, affectionately known as Betsy, the Magic Bus, slowly washing away with the rain. Not entirely though as the wax base remained and held onto dust and grime which made the writing still legible. I was not fazed, although the girls did not care much for being ferried around in a slightly grimy, freedom loving magic bus.

The magic continued for me beyond the bus. My engagement with the shamanic teacher plants of New Zealand kept me occupied. I began to write my journal. We were instructed to keep one as part of the course. Journaling does not come naturally to me. In fact, I find it quite repellent and suffer a huge resistance to writing anything about myself in relation to thoughts and feelings. I can write plans and goals and essays and reflections. I struggle to write thoughts and feelings. Emotions. What a recent revelation. Good grief.

The journal began on the 30th October 2021. The first thing written there is that I had sleep paralysis the night before. That terrifying feeling of being awake, locked inside your body unable to move. I write of my relief that John is coming, that his touch brings me back to my whole self. Dissociation at its finest. I was obviously doing less well than I thought, although unable to see it for myself. I soldiered on regardless. No time for self-pity. No time for any of that nonsense. Get a grip, I told myself.

There is awareness there though. I wrote of being pulled back into old patterns. I can see them. I write of how at home I feel in this shamanic world. I see the dragons in the hills by home. I feel the dragon's breath as one with my own. I stand in ceremony as the ancient lines of the dragons unfold before me. The spirits of the mountains call to me.

Eagle wings are my power symbol. They have always been with me. They give me strength and lift me. I bring my awareness to the natural and spiritual worlds. I listen for the guidance from the plants and animals, and guidance comes. I trust the process.

There is somewhere I took Edie for support on her own journey through this time. I would wait outside and watch the fae in the trees and feel the spirits of the river rocks. I remember sitting and feeling the sun clear and recharge my energy fields. Such a sensation of lightness, joy, and gratitude.

I wrote that I have stopped smoking and drinking. That it has been three weeks. That I am pushing through the cravings whilst being kind to myself and others. Short lived though. I soon picked it up again.

I felt my voice was blocked and I began to sing, "Spirit of the land, I sing to you; spirit of the sea, I sing to you; spirit of the woods, I sing to you." Wherever I roamed, I sang a version of this ditty depending on where I found myself. So simple, and song came back to me. I was finding my soul's voice. I felt a deepening connection to nature and the Universe.

In meditations, which I kept short and sweet, no time to sit and ponder, my body would often move of its own accord, outside of my conscious control. Dragons would come and show me faraway lands. I would ride my horse fast across great deserts and fly high up into the stars where I feel quite at home.

Synchronicities came thick and fast as I was divinely guided through one lunar cycle to the next, always sensing what was to come without having actual access to the next module. Intensely shifting and clearing myself as I went. Old patterns were having layers peeled from them. Realisations were dawning at every turn. It was a time of accelerated learning and personal growth.

Chapter 27

Over the summer, we stayed in a glorious spot on the West Coast. Greenstone retreat in Kumara. Wonderful people, wonderful place. As you turn off the West Coast road at Kumara Junction and head inland between Hokitika and Greymouth towards Arthur's Pass, a truly majestic, mountainous wilderness greets you. The land is not given over to forestry, agriculture, or farming. Native bush prevails. A protected wilderness. The power of the land far exceeding that of tamer Nelson.

The retreat itself alive with the thrum of wildlife was a hive of community activity. Guests encouraged to spend time together in the outside communal kitchen or the healing yoga classes on offer. A sacred divine space where magic was made.

We witnessed the blackest, brightest night skies, and the fieriest sunsets over the powerful ocean. The forests steamed in the heat of the sun, and past summer, the mountains were snow clad. On a clear day they seemed so close you could almost reach out and touch them such was the clarity of the air. A deep settling of my energy overcame me whenever I was there. How could I resist?

On our return to Nelson, I ruminated on my desire to open a

West Coast clinic. This idea had been born soon after our arrival and time spent on the wild West Coast but had been laid to rest over the mandate period. The idea began to grow once more and gather momentum. I contacted Kate who ran the retreat, and between us the Kumara, West Coast clinic was born. I began to travel every three weeks during the mandate time to the coast to run a two-day clinic from Kates yoga studio.

The West Coast has a population of approximately 33,000 people spread over 23,276km^2. The region spans 600km from Kahurangi point in the north to Awarua Point in the south. The healthcare provisions are very limited, and the availability of healthcare professionals is scarce. Folk welcomed me with joy and gratitude.

Each time I turned off the main highway at Kumara Junction with the backdrop of the Southern Alps in my immediate vision, my grin could not get any wider. Only 7km to Kumara village. Time slowed down on the coast, and I could breathe.

The magic bus was wonderful accommodation, even if it took a few visits to perfect the most comfortable sleeping arrangement within her. Getting ready to sleep, I would lay under the watchful gaze of the towering gum forest next to the yoga studio, gazing at the stars and listening to the ocean. Such was the power of the Tasman Sea, where four metre swells are common, that I could sometimes hear it whilst laying in my van at the retreat. It was my safe space during this strange period in history. I felt truly peaceful and held there in that space.

I began to think about the possibility of living on the coast. My first tax return of self-employment had been filed. I earned okay, even during the mandates. I had a little money; $20,000 had been gifted recently from my dad. He had given the same to me and my four siblings after coming into a little money himself, and I had held onto it, which was an amazing feat.

I was determined to put it into something real as the first lockdown had taken most of our $20,000 that we had arrived here with, what was meant to be our yurt money. Buying a van and kitting out our new rental had swallowed the rest.

I had also managed to save $10,000. This was in fact part of my tax bill, but I felt very grown up to have saved it. My life lessons on financial affairs had been non-existent, and it showed. I vowed my financial life as a self-employed osteopath here in New Zealand would be whiter than white. I was a control freak, and I was organised, dagnabbit. I had an accountant, and I had been a very conscientious provisional taxpayer until the mandates hit. I was unsure then if the rug would be completely pulled from under us and as the main breadwinner, I did not want to find ourselves destitute even though I would happily live in a tent, which I mostly did anyway. John was easy, but the children would have moaned for sure.

I rang the tax man and explained my situation: that I was still working and putting money through my books for which I was presumably liable for tax. My immoral earnings as a non-practising osteopath but grey area legal earnings as a healer in hiding. The tax man agreed the situation was unusual but worked out a seven-year payment plan for my grey area tax debt. Anyone that was mandated could apply for tax payment relief. How very gracious.

I found myself in a situation where I had $30,000, the world had gone a bit bonkers, and the ground under our feet was shaky. I decided that if the ground was going to shake, as it often did in New Zealand with frequent earthquakes – a consequence of straddling the Pacific and Australian tectonic plates – that it would be nice to maybe own our own little piece of shaky land. Then if it all went truly belly up, I could take my family and our camping gear and plot up there.

We needed a little more money though. Even with the cheaper land available on the West Coast, $30,000 was not going to cut it. I fished out all the relevant details for John and I and set about applying for personal loans. I did not actually think we would get one. Just to give it our best shot, I applied to Gem Finance for $70,000, the maximum amount they would lend you unsecured. They came back with denied. Computer says no; however, computer says we can borrow $40,000. Mmmmm, okay then. A bit of to-ing and fro-ing, we had used a third-party broker to try to get the maximum possible. Of course we had to pay them a fee, but would we have got it without them? Who knows.

When I say "we", it was really "I". John didn't really know too much other than, "Hey hun, I got us a loan for $40,000, could you just sign here, here, and here. Super job. Thanks babe."

There was a wee plot of 500m2 that had come up in Kumara, it was on for $35,000. We showed our interest, but it had already gone. But then the sale fell through and this time we would have a bit more money to offer. It was put back on the market with sealed bids. Open the envelopes, the highest bid is most likely to win although sometimes they will take a lower bid if the person is able to move quickly, if there are no conditions on the sale, i.e having to sell your own house etc. We were able to move quickly as the loan company had put the money in our account. We put in a bid of $40,000 figuring we would have some money to start work on the land. We were outbid. Madness.

In hindsight, what a blessing. Tiny plots were going for way too much. You could not even walk onto the plot as there was a storm drain running across the front, and a driveway would have to be installed. There was bidding frenzy throughout the coast. People were jumping ship from the main cities and heading west in droves. Land was being snapped up at an alarming rate. Across the social media platforms, adverts were everywhere, people looking for land. Political madness was causing mass exodus.

There were some handwritten signs with phone numbers on selling plots, I heard through the grapevine that so and so was selling a plot. I rung and visited them all. The guy selling off multiple plots had sold all of his barring one. The one he had left he had put the price up way too much. It was a sellers' market for sure.

Another seller was a lovely lady further in the bush on the outskirts of the village. Many folks were retreating to the bush during this time of duress, looking to live a simpler life far from prying eyes. She was so nice but had not yet managed to separate the title on her land. She looked to smoke a zillion cigarettes a day and time was not on her side. Titles took an age to sort in New Zealand and having reassurances that her daughter would sort out everything in the advent of her untimely death was not enough to allay my fears that we would not be left out of pocket.

Then there was the one where we thought we had hit the mark. There was the possibility that a mine would be reopening opposite but, in my excitement, I did not let that sway my judgement. It was close to where I already worked. I was caught up in the frenzy too. The gentleman was looking to sell the 1000m2 plot next to his own with title, $60,000. Handshake. Done. OMG. We thought we had done it. We excitedly took lots of pictures and videos to show the folks back home.

Except when we got back home, the "gentleman" would not return our calls. He did pick up in the end and explained that the neighbours on the other side had seen our excited celebrations and had asked what was going on. Not realising the bare land between them was owned by their neighbour, having never spoken to him before, they promptly made him an offer he could not refuse, and we lost out again. So much for our gentleman's handshake.

Now we had $70,000 and no land. The loan had a two-week let down period where we could return it without incurring a fee. I began to panic. Although $70,000 was a lot of money, it was not a lot of money when looking to purchase land. To put it in perspective, a standard plot of 500–1000m2 in Nelson would be around $380,000 plus and going up all the time. Yikes. I had felt sure we were meant to buy in Kumara but time was running out. We had until the following Wednesday evening to return it before interest began to mount, and on our unsecured personal loan, the interest rate was not pretty.

I headed back down to Kumara for work. I opened my clinic diary. Hang on, who's this? Did she say she was an estate agent? I will commandeer her at the end of her session and ask her advice.

She had come in from Greymouth, 25km away, for her healing (osteo) session. On enquiring if there was any local land she knew for sale she said, "Funny you should ask that, a gentleman rung me from Golden Bay (nearly 400km away) last night and asked if I would be interested in looking at a piece of land in the centre of Kumara that he wishes to sell, and I said to him, 'funny you should ask that as I am heading that way tomorrow for an osteo appointment, I will take a look afterwards.'"

Well, knock me down with a feather. This was it. I was certain. "Are you going now? It's my lunch time, can I come with you?" I asked.

"Sure," she said.

And it was perfect. Slap bang in the middle of the village. No hiding in the bush for us. It was perfect. It was right on the West Coast Wilderness Trail, a stunning four-day cycle ride passing through Kumara, between Ross in the south and Greymouth to the north. Perfect spot for an osteopath. It had a storm drain filled with watercress cutting diagonally across it, but where the estate agent saw a negative, I only saw positives. I knew it had long been a dream for John to build his very own bridge. As she took photos, I could barely contain my excitement.

"Do you think we could put an offer in before it went on the market?" I asked.

She had to check with him, but it came back affirmative. He would look at offers above $55,000. We put in our offer of $60,000 and the vendor accepted the day we were due to hand back our loan. The synchronicities were mind blowing. Don't you just love the Universe.

We were now the proud owners of our very own little piece of West Coast heaven. Just over 1000m2. The Kiwi quintessential quarter acre dream. We had made it. The first time either of us had ever owned anything. Six months into paying off our loan, our statement came through. I was having some trouble getting my head around the figures, so I queried John.

He told me, "That's the interest we paid this month and that's what we paid last month and so on."

Holy mackerel. I do not like adulting. Our little piece of land is going to end up costing a lot more than I thought.

With hindsight, I am not sure that taking out an unsecured personal loan with an extortionate interest rate, adding it to your unpaid tax stash, whilst trying to pay rent in a very expensive town during unstable times where you are deemed to be working illegally, is a very smart move. I do not pretend to give financial advice though. In fact, I am probably the least qualified person to take financial advice from. But doing crazy deeds in an attempt to get ahead, I am good at that. Afterall, there's no growth in the comfort zone.

Chapter 28

The mandates for the health sector dropped late September 2022, and I could "officially" call myself an osteopath again. I had taken it upon myself to reclaim my osteopathic title earlier than decreed and was a registered osteopath and ACC provider once more, much earlier than many of my colleagues. Some never reclaimed their title. Such a huge loss. I, though, was already up and running having started the process in June.

Societal pressure was easing. I needed to think about my life. I was still drinking and smoking, and as much as I liked to think I had it all under control, it was a fallacy. Because I am an alcoholic, and alcohol is insidious. It creeps up on you until you are once again powerless to resist. I did not wish to find myself there again. I knew change was upon me. The right time was approaching.

After opening the West Coast clinic, I realised I was enjoying driving the country in my trusty old van, Betsy, the Magic Bus. Getting out of Nelson and away from the madness was good for my soul. I had some folks who were travelling across Arthur's Pass, traversing the Southern Alps from Christchurch on the East Coast to see me on the West Coast, a six hour round trip. So I hatched a plan: I would set up a clinic on the East Coast in Rangiora near to Christchurch and drive over Arthurs Pass. I would then drive home north to Nelson through Lewis Pass. A spectacular 908km round trip of alpine mountain pass epicness every three weeks. My first clinic in Rangiora was early November 2022. I vowed to see how it went; if it would be too much of a toll being away from my family for one week out of every three then I would not continue after Christmas.

A beautiful spot in Rangiora called The Sanctuary welcomed me with open arms. A hub for healing activity, food, forests, and alternative tiny home living. I immediately felt part of their fabulous community. And would you believe it, on arrival, a lovely lady that lived there stopped me on her way out, she recognised me from somewhere and it transpired that she was one of the moderators for the shamanic course I was taking.

"I always look forward to your classroom posts," she told me. How randomly synchronous. How divine.

So now I had a clinic in Nelson, a clinic in Kumara, and a clinic in Rangiora, and as I drove between them I got to venture through these amazing mountain passes. Arthur's Pass is situated between Kumara and Rangiora and is the highest pass of the Southern Alps, sitting at 900m. Climbing up to the pass where you regularly see Kea, the famous New Zealand alpine parrot (notorious for chewing your wiper blades off your car or pinching your lunch if you stop in Arthur's Pass village), includes driving the spectacular Otira Viaduct. A 445m cantilevered bridge snaking its way through the mountains. Huge drop offs either side would make my sphincter contract, and I kept my eyes firmly on the road, my hands gripping the steering wheel as my feet sweated. It is not advisable to tow trailers over the viaduct. It is steep and prone to earthquakes and huge rainfall events causing landslips. It has become easier to traverse, less sphincter contracting the more I have done it.

Lewis Pass, between Rangiora and Nelson, is much tamer in comparison. It follows the wide valleys of the Lewis and Maruia rivers. The road can be narrow and winds up through clouded forest to the pass which sits at 865m and is the northernmost pass of the Southern Alps. It is far less scary to traverse. But both are stunning.

As I drove from Kumara one time, heading east, I stopped at a quirky hotel in Otira for a coffee, the Otira Stagecoach Hotel. An absolute gem, jam packed with quirky memorabilia and ephemera. The gentleman, Lester, that ran the place was quirky, too. It quickly came to his attention that I was an osteopath and blessed be because he had a sore shoulder. So, in front of a roaring fire, between bites of my slightly stale but revived cheesy scone, I worked on his shoulder.

We must have made quite a sight; a few Japanese tourists began to take photos of us. On completion of his flyby treatment, Lester gifted me some Otira honey and some interesting yet out of date Otira calendars. He also recommended that I add Otira to my list of clinics, I could work from one of the rooms in the hotel. He had treatment couches, etc, set up out back that were not being used.

I was severely tempted but this was getting out of hand now. I had to see my family at some point. Being a Sagittarius, born the year of the horse and a life path number 7, my desire for adventure was high and temptation was strong. I would happily galivant all over the country touting my wares. I had to reign myself in though. At this point in my life, my family needed me too, and as easy as John is, he might not be too happy being left to hold all the proverbial babies.

⇒ ★ ⇐

It soon became apparent that although I would not continue to make this journey, destiny decreed that I had to make a particular one. I needed this moment in time, and it came just before Christmas.

As I came through Lewis Pass in December of 2022, enjoying the sunshine and marvelling at the large black dragon that resides in the mountains there, a parchment and quill dropped into my awareness, not of my own will or imagination. As I drove, the quill began to auto write. It was happening all by itself, not of my conscious control, and I could not stop it. It wrote individual letters to each of my siblings and to my parents. The exact nature of these letters I could not replicate but they detailed the angst, the fears and worries of a young girl that did not know how to deal with her emotions appropriately and for which she had no guidance. A young girl that had repressed her emotions for a long time. A girl that needed to feel these emotions and not shut them out. They detailed the apologies she needed to make and the forgiveness of herself and others. The quill did not stop until it was done. With each letter completed a lifting and clearing of my system was felt. I was becoming lighter. More transparent. A spiritual cleansing that came to pass in Lewis Pass. It came as a gift from the Divine. The gift of forgiveness and self-love. An inner child healing from the place of infinite light.

It was now time to get myself together. I had clearly just had an amazing healing experience, and I wanted to keep moving forward with my own healing. I needed to stop drinking. I needed to focus on my two main clinics. I was stretching myself too thin and putting myself and family under too much pressure by continuing the Rangiora clinic, but I truly believe that it was necessary for me to be there in that moment to experience the healing that I did. A healing that transported me back in time to myself, aged 10, the point of shattered innocence and the catalyst for what would follow. A tumultuous path of lost connection and addiction that enabled me to pass through the many rites of passage needed to elevate me to the divine powerful healing channel that I am today. I will remain forever grateful for my path in life.

Chapter 29

The girls went back to the UK over Christmas to see Gary and family. He had already made it over for ten weeks earlier in the year – he had come as soon as the borders opened and stayed with us. That was an emotional reunion, subject to much partying and celebration alongside cycling, kayaking, hiking, and swimming with our girls. Gary got to experience the New Zealand he had heard so much about but had been kept so far from. We missed him when he returned to the UK but we hoped to resume our original plan for time together now that the world had calmed down.

Although we would have liked to, we could not afford for all of us to go back to the UK, so John, Walker, and I walked the Old Ghost Road instead. An amazing 85km of forest, alpine, and river valley environs delivering us to the West Coast close to where we were spending New Year with friends.

A long walk was the most perfect way to integrate such a powerful healing. To be far out in the wilds walking through powerful landscapes between huts; carrying all our food and equipment for four nights and five days in the bush. It was summer in New Zealand, but the weather can be very changeable in the mountains. Our first day starting in the upper Buller Gorge some two and a half hours from Nelson saw us climbing straight up 16km with heavy packs being pelted with hail. Walker marvelled. I do not think he had seen hail before and he positively ran the last 5km, usually the point he is tiring, skipping gaily through the forming puddles. His good mood continued unabated when Santa made a visit to that first hut.

Much to the surprise of the other hut guests who were all mountain bikers, we carried in fresh vegetables, trusty salami (a backpacking staple), gravy, and a fruit cake, and had Christmas dinner at the next hut, Ghost Lake. It sits at 1205m at the top of a towering east facing cliff. The sunrise the next morning over peaks as far as the eye can see rising out of the ethereal cloud inversion is another memory bank moment. The stillness only broken by the theft of someone's wallet from their bike by a cheeky weka.

That day saw us walk the spine of the ridge known as skyline ridge, a slim precipitous ridge in the midst of 360-degree forest clad mountainous panorama. It was a beautiful, hot, clear day and we kept the pace up so that we may be off the ridge before the heat of the midday sun. At the end of the ridge, we climbed down the infamous skyline steps, a manmade marvel of winding wooden steps to fetch you from the skies down into the forest below, and into the next high valley where we would be staying and enjoying a cool river swim whilst trying to avoid the sandflies who delighted in our presence.

We rose early on what would be our longest day yet at 25km, and the weather was scorching. We had to pass through an area known as the Boneyard, an earthquake shattered area of towering white rocks that reflect the midday sun and scorched you like a wee ant under glass if you are foolish enough to be caught walking through after noon. This day took us twelve hours with many stops for tea, noodles, and river swimming. Walker got a big round of applause when we trudged into Specimen Point Hut that night, his fellow travellers amazed at his epic feat.

The last day saw us follow the Mohikinui River to Seddonville on the West Coast. A lush winding gorge of crystal-clear waters, white sandy banks, and high, wobbly suspension bridges. Walker and I were discussing owls and how they can turn their heads so far in either direction, and as we turned the next corner, low and behold, right there in front of us was a little morepork, or ruru as it is known here, the last remaining New Zealand native owl. He was roosting in the thick vegetation. His eyes popped open, and he graciously demonstrated his amazing neck bending abilities. It felt like he was there just for us. Thank you, little owl.

Although we were happy to be heading out, it was tinged with a deep sadness. It is always sad to leave the trail behind. You get into such a natural rhythm, nothing else matters and the hectic manner of daily life falls far behind you. You are at one with yourself, nature, and the Universe. The breath of life moved in and out of me, expanding and contracting through me as I plodded along. Yes, I would be sad to leave this place.

To ease our transition back to civilisation we walked out of Old Ghost Road straight into the Rough and Tumble Lodge still deep in the bush and celebrated with pizza and beers. The king size beds were heavenly as were the bathrooms and laundry facilities. Nothing will beat the roast dinner though, laid on in the evening for hikers staying who have finished the trail. Magnificent does not come close. John ate three full size plates; I managed two; Walker had a good sized one. We all managed pudding of course. We slept very well that night.

 The next day we collected our van which had been relocated for us. This is a common thing in New Zealand where many trails are single tracks that pop you out far from your starting point. We had on board all of our camping equipment and headed off to meet our friends at the stunning campground, Gentle Annie at Mokihinui where we had enjoyed nearly every New Year since we arrived in New Zealand, and which was responsible for starting our love of the West Coast. We camped right at the mouth of the river we had been following the day before. It is hard to describe the landscape, I have run out of words to do it justice, but "Jurassic" is a good word for conjuring up the image. I was overcome with emotion.

 With high running emotions comes much frivolity, and I enjoyed a very debauched New Year. Staying up partying until sunrise whilst John and Walker slept soundly in our tent. The experience of the last three years, my girls being so far from me, and our epic stomp through the mountains all came to a head, and I really let loose. I drank it, ate it, smoked it, and sniffed it. If it was offered, I took it. A complete blowout. Fun at the time but painful, alarming, and regretful the next day. Feelings I knew only too well.

 You might think that would be the end of the drinking for me, but I wasn't quite yet done. We headed back to Nelson soon after, driving east again via Christchurch to pick the girls up from the airport. They had travelled to the UK and back all by themselves, aged 14 and 15. I could not be prouder of them. What an achievement. They are quite blasé about flying now. The heady heights of Dubai so excitedly raved over on their way out now a mere blip in their quest to get home. Yes, they now viewed New

Zealand as home they told me. They wanted to get back to Nelson. They still had a few weeks of summer to enjoy with their friends. That was quite a moment. My heart sang to hear it. It had been tough going at times.

The final blowout came with the change in the leadership of New Zealand mid-January 2023. I saw it as the metaphorical end of a troublesome period, the pandemic which had plagued our lives since landing in New Zealand was on its way out and taking with it all its divisive acts. It was now time to really begin experiencing New Zealand as it was before. A time to live our lives in the New Zealand of my youthful dreams and student musings; when I qualify, I'm going to be an osteopath in New Zealand.

Well, I bloody made it. This stinky bird made it. You can too.

Epilogue

The following Monday I took myself off to the quintessential church room circle depicted so beautifully in films referencing alcoholics. I introduced myself and spoke *those* ten little words out loud to a bunch of perfect strangers and it was so *liberating*. Who knew ten words could be so liberating. Freedom was mine at last. Then I cried and cried and cried. Years of tears I cried. Boy, did it feel good.

Through my long hard dance with addiction over the years, I have been supported in my quest for sobriety in all manner of ways. There are some fantastic support groups on social media, they are not hard to find. There is a multitude of quitting literature affectionately known as quit lit available to you. I have utilised these over the years as I struggled to understand and work through my addiction. Great resources. There are the traditional groups that meet and sit in a circle, so scary at first but soon to become your comfort blanket. If you are struggling, I highly encourage you to reach out. Reach out to someone. Recovery starts with you. You have to take the first step. Take the first step in reclaiming your true self; that magical special being that only you can be. The world needs you.

At the time of writing, I realise as I check my app counter for the purpose of this book that I have been alcohol free for 1 year, 1 month, and 16 days. It's not something I look at daily. I am just happy to be free.

My life remains exciting, my clinic room is gathering quite the variety of helpers from different dimensions. I continue to level up at pace, gathering superpowers as I continue to heal facets of myself. I still have three sets of wings and I regularly see others release theirs through treatment. It is an exciting time to be alive.

We have our land on the West Coast which we are in the process of having plans drawn up for. It will be on the tiny alternative side. I've no idea how we will afford it, but I see in my field that it eventuates, so I continue to trust the Universe has my back even if my bank account doesn't appear to. There is always just enough though, and I'm sure abundance is just around the corner. Wink face.

I put my big girl pants on and took my clinic back into town. It is nice to play with other grown-ups again. I have the best of both worlds at present, working from home and the city. A beautiful lesson in trusting others once more and being able to let go and move on.

I have started to write the prequel to this book, I have made a good start. I was overcome one weekend with the need to begin even though I had not yet finished this book. I stayed in bed for two days solid. The words flying out of my digital pen. I cried and railed, snotty, red, and puffy as I wrote. John tiptoeing around me, only coming in to bring me more food. I collapsed with exhaustion at the end. The feeling of toxic overload quite overwhelming. Another huge release. I felt emotionally hungover for days after. This writing lark is quite cathartic. I should do it more often.

I shall have a wee break and then pick it up again and try to make legible sense of it. Then maybe the sequel. I've got to live a little more first. I'm sure there are still plenty of adventures to be had. Who knows what will eventuate. Only time and the Universe will tell.

Last of all, happy healing folks. And if it's not feeling particularly joyous right now, just remember: the darkest night of your soul is the springboard to your magical authentic self.

Make the jump. Reach for the stars. Who knows how far you'll go.

www.ingramcontent.com/pod-product-compliance
Lightning Source LLC
Chambersburg PA
CBHW062054290426
44109CB00027B/2826